AS/A-LEVEL

19th & 20th Century British History

Graham Goodlad

ESSENTIAL WORD
DICTIONARY

In memory of my grandfather Astley Lee Goodlad, 1899–1985

Philip Allan Updates
Market Place
Deddington
Oxfordshire
OX15 0SE

Tel: 01869 338652
Fax: 01869 337590
e-mail: sales@philipallan.co.uk
www.philipallan.co.uk

ISBN 0 86003 380 5

Printed by Raithby, Lawrence & Co Ltd, Leicester

Introduction

This *Essential Word Dictionary* will provide you with invaluable information to use as you prepare for the AS or A2 examinations. (The specific modules/units covered are listed in an appendix — see pages 148–149.) To succeed at these examinations you need to:

- have a sound **knowledge and understanding of history**. This means being able to recall, select and deploy historical knowledge accurately.
- be able to evaluate **sources in historical context**. This means having knowledge of the topic on which the source is based.
- be able to explain **different historical interpretations.** A new feature of A2 History is **synoptic assessment**. This involves bringing together in one answer different aspects of history. One of these aspects could be the role of the individual.
- display good written communication skills. This is also an important part of **Basic Key Skills**, and includes the ability to use historical terms accurately.

This dictionary will enable you to deal effectively with all these features of the AS and A2 examinations. Included in the dictionary are entries on:

- major historical events such as wars and treaties.
- important historical terms such as balance of power.
- key historical figures.

The dictionary can be used:

- to define historical terms. These are required in dealing with document questions and in extended writing such as essays.
- to help you to understand a particular topic.
- as a revision aid.

To use the dictionary as a revision aid, first compile a checklist of essential terms, events and individuals you need for an examination. Look these terms up in the dictionary and then learn and understand them so that you can use them with confidence in the examination.

Each entry is broken down into a maximum of three parts:

(1) A simple definition is given after the headword.

(2) This is followed by a series of bullet points which place important events in historical context.

(3) An examiner's tip is then included where appropriate. These tips are intended to help you to use the entries in your studies. They include references to common misunderstandings about the entry or offer advice on how to use the terms in preparation for examinations.

For each entry it may be necessary to make a cross-reference to the words in italics in order to understand fully the entry you are reading.

This title is one of a series of *Essential Word Dictionaries*, which includes a companion volume on *AS/A-Level 19th and 20th Century European and World History*.

Abdication Crisis, 1936: the events leading up to the decision of King Edward VIII to give up the throne in favour of his younger brother, who became George VI.

- Edward had made known his intention to marry an American divorcee, Wallis Simpson. This was unacceptable to public opinion in Britain and in the *Dominions*. He had to abdicate the throne in December 1936 in order to marry Mrs Simpson.
- The crisis was smoothly handled by *Baldwin* as Prime Minister. It demonstrated his ability to interpret the mood of the British people and Parliament.

Aberdeen (George Hamilton Gordon), 4th Earl of (1784–1860): British Foreign Secretary 1828–30, 1841–46; Prime Minister 1852–55.

- As Foreign Secretary in the 1840s, Aberdeen built good relations with France and the USA, in contrast to the more aggressive style of *Palmerston*. He followed *Peel* in the crisis over the repeal of the *Corn Laws* in 1846.
- He led a *coalition* government of *Whigs* and *Peelites* that was brought down following criticism of his handling of the *Crimean War*. Aberdeen was not an inspired war leader.

  TIP Exam questions on British foreign policy in the mid-nineteenth century, or on the Crimean War, require a knowledge of Aberdeen's career.

Abyssinian expedition, 1867–68: a military mission launched by the *Derby* government to rescue Western hostages held by King Theodore of Abyssinia (now known as Ethiopia).

- The expedition has been seen by some historians as an example of a new kind of *imperialism* on the part of British governments. *Disraeli*, the dominant figure in the government, has been held responsible for it. In fact, British troops were withdrawn once the prisoners had been released and national pride satisfied. There was no take-over of territory.

Abyssinian War, 1935–36: caused by the Italian leader Mussolini's invasion of Abyssinia (now known as Ethiopia).

- British interests were affected because the area was close to the Suez Canal, jointly controlled by Britain and France.
- Sir Samuel Hoare, British Foreign Secretary in the *Baldwin* government, tried

to end the war in December 1935 by a secret deal with French Prime Minister Pierre Laval. The Hoare–Laval Pact, which would have handed over large parts of Abyssinia to Italy, became known to the British public. It was widely condemned and Hoare had to resign.

▩ *TIP* This is an example of the policy of *appeasement* followed by British governments in their dealings with European dictators in the 1930s.

Act of Union, 1800: an act that ended Ireland's separate Parliament and created the United Kingdom of Great Britain and Ireland.

● The act was passed by *Pitt*'s government. It gave Ireland 105 MPs at Westminster and some representation in the House of Lords. Irish government was run from Dublin Castle and headed by a Viceroy (Lord Lieutenant), who represented the British monarchy. A *Cabinet* minister, the Chief Secretary for Ireland, was also appointed.

● This system of government continued down to the *Anglo–Irish Treaty, 1921.* It was opposed by the *Irish National Party.*

▩ *TIP* The key features of the Act of Union are important for an understanding of the *Irish Question.*

Addington, Henry: see *Sidmouth, Viscount.*

Adullamites: right-wing Liberal rebels who were against *Russell*'s 1866 bill to extend the vote to sections of the working class.

● The name is derived from a reference in the Bible to a group that hid in the Cave of Adullam.

● These MPs believed that working-class people had not yet been educated for the responsibilities of voting. They joined with the Conservative opposition to defeat the Russell government.

▩ *TIP* The Adullamites are an example of the difficulties faced by nineteenth-century Liberal leaders in maintaining the unity of their party, which consisted of a number of different groups.

Afghan Wars, 1878–79: wars caused by the belief of Lord Lytton, Viceroy (British ruler) of India, that Britain must occupy Afghanistan in order to protect India against a possible Russian invasion.

● Afghanistan was situated on the northwest frontier of Britain's Indian empire, to the south of Russia.

● The invasion went badly for Britain and members of a military expedition were massacred in the capital, Kabul. This reflected badly on the *Disraeli* government and contributed to its defeat in the 1880 general election, even though it had little direct control over events. The troops were withdrawn in 1880.

▩ *TIP* The wars illustrate the difficulties of communication faced by governments in supervising the *British empire* in the nineteenth century.

***agent provocateur*:** an undercover agent, employed by governments before the introduction of the police force, who infiltrated groups suspected of illegal or treasonable activities.

- The Metropolitan Police Force was not introduced until 1829 and some parts of the country did not have a police force for another 20 years. This meant that governments at the beginning of the nineteenth century continued to rely on older methods of law enforcement.
- Such an agent would work his way into a group being investigated by the authorities and encourage them to start some trouble. This would provide an opportunity for the members of the group to be arrested.
- The most notorious agent was W. J. Richards (known as 'Oliver the spy'), who helped to foil the *Pentrich Rising, 1817*.

age of austerity: the period of the 1945–51 Labour government, when wartime rationing and restrictions were still in force.

- *Attlee*'s Labour government aimed to create a fairer, more equal society by reducing the amount spent by individuals on private consumption and by directing resources towards industrial production and new welfare services. Austerity was particularly associated with Sir Stafford Cripps, who emphasised the theme of personal sacrifice as Chancellor of the Exchequer from 1947 to 1950.
- From about 1947, the policy became increasingly unpopular, especially with housewives, who resented rationing and queues. It played a part in the return to power of the *Conservative Party* in 1951.
- *TIP* Exam questions on the domestic policies of the Attlee governments will require a knowledge of the key features of 'austerity' policies.

Agricultural Depression, 1873–1914: serious economic problems facing British agriculture, especially wheat farming.

- The depression was caused by competition from farmers in North America and by heavy rainfall in the late 1870s, which damaged cereal crops. Refrigerated meat imports from South America, Australia and New Zealand also affected livestock farmers. British governments were committed to *free trade* and did little to help farmers.
- As a result of the depression, many farmers turned to alternative sources of income, such as market gardening.
- *TIP* Historians of the late-Victorian economy are divided as to how seriously trade and industry were affected by the depression, but there is no doubt that agriculture suffered badly.

Agricultural Revolution: a movement in eighteenth-century Britain to introduce more efficient methods in farming.

- The enclosing of arable land with hedges and fences was one of the main features of the revolution in central and southern England. This enabled the introduction of the four-course crop rotation, whereby land used for cereal crops had its fertility restored by growing root crops (e.g. turnips) in alternate years.
- Selective breeding of livestock, to produce a better quality of meat, was also developed.
- The importance of these changes was that they enabled British agriculture to

feed a growing population which, by 1800, was beginning to move towards the towns and cities of the *Industrial Revolution*.

Alabama Claims: claims for damages against the British government, made by the USA after the American Civil War (1861–65) and finally settled by *Gladstone* in 1872.

● The *Alabama* was a ship, built in Britain and used by the Southern (Confederate) side to raid the Northern merchant fleet during the Civil War. The US government claimed £9m in damages, arguing that Britain had broken its commitment to neutrality during the war.

● Gladstone submitted the case to international arbitration (the judgement of a neutral court). The court awarded the USA damages of £3.25m and Gladstone paid up.

● This was used by the Conservatives as evidence of Liberal weakness in standing up for British interests.

▨ *TIP* The episode is a useful illustration of differences between Gladstone and *Disraeli* in foreign affairs.

Alliance: see *Social Democratic Party (SDP)*.

Amritsar massacre, 1919: an incident that occurred in the capital of the Punjab, in northern India, when British General Dyer ordered troops to fire on a crowd of demonstrators.

● The massacre claimed the lives of some 300 unarmed people and helped to make British rule in India unpopular, stimulating the growth of Indian nationalism. The British government relieved Dyer of his post following the massacre.

Andover workhouse scandal, 1846: a case of particularly distressing conditions experienced by the inmates of a workhouse in Hampshire, which led to a reorganisation of the *New Poor Law*.

● It was revealed that inmates of the Andover workhouse had been starved under the harsh regime imposed by the local board of guardians. They had been ordered to crush animal bones for fertiliser production and had been reduced to eating the bone marrow.

● The subsequent outcry led to the dissolution of the Poor Law Commission, the central body created to supervise the Poor Law in 1834. It was replaced by a Poor Law Board, headed by a minister who was answerable to Parliament.

▨ *TIP* The scandal is an important turning point in the history of Poor Law administration.

Anglican Church: the religion officially recognised by the state as the Established Church, with the monarch as its Supreme Governor. In England, it corresponds to the Church of England.

● At the beginning of the nineteenth century, Anglicanism was the official religion of Wales and Ireland as well as England. The Anglican Church, which was created in the sixteenth century after the monarchy rejected the authority of the Pope, was run by bishops. In Scotland, the Established Church remains the Presbyterian (non-Anglican) Church of Scotland.

- The privileged position of the Anglican Church created resentment among *nonconformists*, many of whom wanted to see it disestablished, so giving all denominations an equal status. This was achieved in Ireland in 1869 and in Wales in 1920.

Anglo–Boer War, 1880–81: a conflict between Britain and the Boers (Afrikaners), a race of Dutch settlers who had established themselves in southern Africa.

- The war of 1880–81 broke out when Boer leaders, who had expected Britain to allow them independence, lost patience and defeated a British force at Majuba Hill. The Pretoria Convention was then signed, giving independence to the Boer republic of the Transvaal, apart from British supervision of its foreign relationships.

Anglo–Boer War, 1899–1902 (also known as the 'Boer War' or 'South African War')**:** a second and more important conflict than the war of 1880–81 between Britain and the Boer settlers of southern Africa.

- Some historians see it as a war over the gold and diamond resources of the region. Others argue that it was caused by Britain's desire to dominate the strategically important southern tip of Africa and to maintain its prestige as a *Great Power*.
- The war eventually resulted in a British victory and the incorporation of the Boer republics of the Transvaal and Orange Free State into the British empire.
- *TIP* The difficulties faced by Britain in winning the war caused an important debate about Britain's world role and strength as a Great Power (the *national efficiency* debate). You should be familiar with the consequences of the war, both domestic and international, as well as with its causes.

Anglo–French Agreement, 1904 (also known as 'Entente Cordiale')**:** a settlement of disputes between Britain and France over colonial issues, which paved the way for co-operation between the two in face of growing German power.

- The agreement recognised Britain's control of Egypt and France's special position of influence in Morocco, which had been disputed since the 1880s. It was not intended to be a firm alliance and was not at first directed against Germany.
- *TIP* The significance of the agreement for Britain's relations with European powers is important for exam questions on the ending of *splendid isolation*.

Anglo–German Naval Agreement, 1935: an agreement that allowed Nazi Germany to build a navy up to one third of the size of Britain's Royal Navy.

- The agreement was signed without reference to Britain's main European ally, France. It is an example of the *appeasement* of Hitler's Germany.

Anglo–Irish Agreement, 1985 (also known as the 'Hillsborough Agreement')**:** an agreement signed by British Prime Minister Margaret *Thatcher* with Irish Prime Minister Garret Fitzgerald, in an attempt to bring stability to Northern Ireland.

- The agreement was a response to growing support for *Sinn Fein* and to republican terrorist violence in Northern Ireland. It involved the government of the Irish Republic in discussions with the British government on matters of common concern, such as cross-border security. The Irish government accepted that Northern Ireland would remain British as long as a majority of the population there wished it.

- It was rejected by the Unionist community in Northern Ireland because it allowed the Irish government a say in the government of part of the UK.

Anglo–Irish ascendancy: the landowning class, members of the *Anglican Church,* who dominated Irish society between the sixteenth century and the partition of Ireland in 1921.

- Members of the ascendancy were descended from Protestant settlers who had taken land in Ireland from the native Catholic population. They were powerful in local government, the armed forces and the justice system.

   ■ *TIP* In exam questions on the *Irish Question* in the nineteenth century, be able to explain why the ascendancy was unpopular with the Catholic community.

Anglo–Irish Treaty, 1921: an agreement between the British government and representatives of the Irish republican *Sinn Fein* movement. Ireland was to be divided between a practically independent Irish Free State in the South and Northern Ireland (Ulster), which was to remain within the UK.

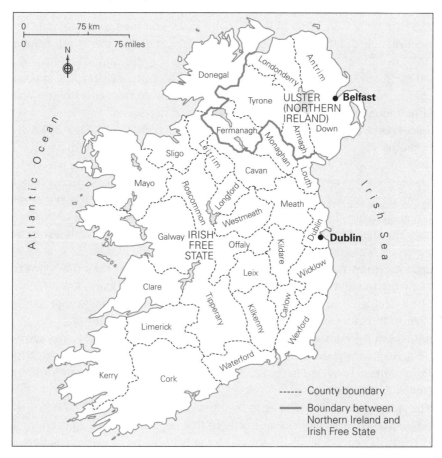

- The treaty brought to an end the Anglo–Irish conflict of 1919–21, fought by the *Lloyd George* government against the *IRA*. The treaty was a compromise between the desire of Ulster to remain associated with Britain and the demand for independence expressed by a majority in Southern Ireland. The Irish Free State was given the status of a British *Dominion*, staying technically within the *British empire.*
- The treaty was rejected by some republicans and a violent civil war was fought in the South between supporters and opponents in 1922–23.
- *TIP* The terms of the treaty are very important for any exam question on twentieth-century Ireland.

Anglo–Japanese alliance, 1902: an agreement between Britain and Japan to support each other if either was attacked in the Far East by more than one enemy power.

- The alliance was negotiated by British Foreign Secretary *Lansdowne* and has sometimes been seen as the first break with a nineteenth-century tradition of *splendid isolation* from foreign commitments. Critics saw it as an encouragement to Japan to go to war with its main rival, Russia, in 1904.
- The alliance was renewed in 1905 and provided the main basis of British policy in the Far East until the 1920s.

Anti-Corn Law League: a large and well-organised pressure group founded in Manchester in 1838 to campaign for the removal of taxes on wheat.

- The league was founded by Richard *Cobden* and John Bright. It commanded strong support in manufacturing towns, where high food prices kept the cost of living high for the industrial and merchant population.
- It made good use of the national postal service (started in 1840) and the railways to spread its message.
- *TIP* The league must be considered in exam questions on the repeal (abolition) of the *Corn Laws*. It was not, however, the main factor in the decision of *Peel's* government to do away with the laws.

appeasement: a policy of making concessions to a potentially hostile power in order to secure peace.

- The term is commonly used to describe the attitude of British governments in the 1930s towards Hitler's Germany and Mussolini's Italy.
- The policy has been much criticised for showing weakness in the face of aggression, although in recent years historians have tended to take a more favourable view. It was based on an awareness of the financial and human costs of risking another world war.
- Examples of appeasement include the *Anglo–German Naval Agreement, 1935* and the *Munich Agreement, 1938.*
- *TIP* In answering questions on British foreign policy in the 1930s, be prepared to assess the case for and against the appeasement of Germany and Italy.

Arrow incident, 1856: a diplomatic incident between Britain and China, after the Chinese authorities arrested the crew of the ***Arrow***, a British-registered ship.

- The background to the incident was the dislike of the Chinese for foreign interference, and the desire of British merchants to open up the region to trade.
- The British governor of Hong Kong ordered the bombardment of Canton in retaliation for the seizure of the crew. He was supported by *Palmerston*, the Prime Minister. Although the action was condemned in the House of Commons, the British public approved strong action against foreigners and this helped Palmerston win the 1857 general election.
- The affair led to the second of the *Opium Wars.*

▓ *TIP* In answering questions on Palmerston's foreign policy, the incident is a good illustration of a common charge against him, that he acted aggressively against weaker states.

Artisans' Dwellings Act, 1875: one of the social reforms of the 1874–80 *Disraeli* government that enabled local authorities to pull down slum housing.

- The term 'artisan' means a member of the skilled working class, a craftsman who had served an apprenticeship. Many working-class people were living in unhealthy, poor-quality housing in the industrial cities.
- The act invited private firms to build new houses to replace the slums. It is an example of *permissive legislation* (non-compulsory legislation).
- The costs to ratepayers meant that few local councils made use of it. A notable exception was *Joseph Chamberlain*, who rebuilt central Birmingham as Mayor in the mid-1870s.

Ashdown, Paddy (1941–): leader of the *Liberal Democrat Party* from 1988 to 1999, who steered his party towards co-operation with the *Labour Party*.

- MP for Yeovil in Somerset, he was the first leader of the Liberal Democrat Party, formed from the merger of the *Liberal Party* and the *Social Democratic Party (SDP).*
- He found common ground with *Blair*'s New Labour policies and abandoned the traditional postwar Liberal stance of equal distance between Labour and the Conservatives. After the 1997 general election, in which the Liberal Democrats won 46 seats, Ashdown was rewarded with a place on a *Cabinet* committee on constitutional reform.

Asquith, Herbert Henry (1852–1928): Home Secretary 1892–95, Chancellor of the Exchequer 1905–08, Prime Minister 1908–16, leader of the *Liberal Party* 1908–26.

- Asquith led the Liberal government that introduced social reforms, such as *old age pensions* and *National Insurance*, and passed the *Parliament Act*, which limited the powers of the *House of Lords* following the constitutional crisis of 1909–11.
- He took Britain into the First World War in August 1914. In May 1915, he formed a *coalition* with the *Conservative Party* and the *Labour Party.*
- He was regarded as a weak wartime leader, and in December 1916 he was replaced as Prime Minister by *Lloyd George*. This initiated a damaging split in the Liberal Party and Asquith did not regain his authority in the 1920s.

Attlee, Clement (1883–1967): Chancellor of the Duchy of Lancaster 1930–31; Postmaster General 1931; Deputy Prime Minister 1940–45; leader of the *Labour Party* 1935–55, who headed the first majority Labour administration as Prime Minister from 1945 to 1951.

- Attlee was a quietly efficient Prime Minister, with a deceptively modest public image. He was an effective deputy prime minister to *Winston Churchill* during the Second World War before winning the 1945 general election.
- The Attlee governments introduced the *welfare state*, including the *National Health Service* in 1948.
- His governments introduced widespread *nationalisation,* including important industries such as coal, gas, electricity and railways.
- He began the break-up of the *British empire*. In 1947, India and Pakistan received independence, followed by Ceylon (now known as Sri Lanka) and Burma in 1948.
- Under his leadership, Britain became a close ally of the USA in the *Cold War* against the USSR, taking the decision to build a British atomic bomb and helping to found the *North Atlantic Treaty Organisation (NATO)* in 1949.
- Attlee narrowly won the 1950 general election, but lost to the Conservatives under Churchill in 1951.

balance of payments: the difference between a country's income from foreign countries and its payments to those countries.

- A balance of payments crisis occurs when the money earned from exports is less than the money a country spends on imports from abroad.
- Britain had a severe crisis of this kind after the Second World War. This was a result of the huge cost of the war, combined with the Labour government's spending on welfare reforms at home. The government was forced to introduce import controls and other tough measures in 1947 in order to overcome the crisis.

balance of power: a concept in diplomatic history — the idea that peace would be best preserved if no single power was strong enough to threaten the rest of Europe.

- This meant that Britain would co-operate with other European powers in order to find peaceful solutions to problems. This co-operation was known in the nineteenth century as the 'Concert of Europe'. An example was the period 1815–23, when Britain participated in congresses (meetings of the foreign ministers of the main European powers).
- Sometimes Britain went to war in order to maintain the balance of power — in the *Crimean War* to restrain Russia and in the First World War against Germany.
- *TIP* You should be able to define 'balance of power' and give examples of British action in its defence.

Baldwin, Stanley (1867–1947): Chancellor of the Exchequer 1922–23; Prime Minister 1923–24, 1924–29, 1935–37; leader of the *Conservative Party* 1923–37.

- He emerged from relative obscurity when he helped to lead the *Carlton Club revolt*, which ended the *Lloyd George coalition* government.
- As Conservative leader, Baldwin projected a reassuring, moderate image, stressing national unity at a time of labour unrest and economic depression. He was the first politician to make effective use of radio and film media.
- He played an important part in defeating the *General Strike, 1926* and creating the *National Government*.
- He was criticised for his alleged slowness to rearm the country in the 1930s against the threat of Nazi Germany.

■ *TIP* Watch out for exam questions which ask for an assessment of Baldwin's achievements as Prime Minister and those which focus on his role as leader of the Conservative Party — two different angles.

Balfour, Arthur, Earl Balfour (1848–1930): Chief Secretary for Ireland 1887–91; Leader of the *House of Commons* 1891–92, 1895–1902; Prime Minister 1902–05; leader of the *Conservative Party* 1902–11; Foreign Secretary 1916–19.

● He was an ineffective Prime Minister, who failed to maintain party unity during the controversy over *tariff reform*. He lost the 1906 general election heavily to the Liberals.

● As Conservative leader in opposition, he was regarded as insufficiently aggressive in dealing with the Liberal government.

● As Foreign Secretary, he made the 1917 Balfour declaration, in which Britain declared its support for a 'national home' for the Jewish people in Palestine (now Israel).

● He served in the postwar *Lloyd George coalition* and again in *Baldwin*'s 1924–29 Conservative government.

■ *TIP* Balfour was a central figure in the decline of Conservative Party fortunes in 1900–06.

Bank Charter Act, 1844: a measure to stabilise the economy by restricting the issue of banknotes.

● Previously banks had had unlimited power to issue banknotes. Many banks collapsed in financial crises because their paper money was not backed by gold reserves.

● The Bank Charter Act was introduced by *Peel*'s government in order to restore investors' confidence in the banking system. It gave the Bank of England greater control over the issue of notes and limited their issue by other banks.

Battle of Britain, 1940: a series of air battles over southern England, fought between the RAF and the German Luftwaffe, which frustrated Hitler's planned invasion of Britain.

● To carry out his invasion plan (codenamed 'Operation Sealion'), Hitler had to win control of the air space over southern England. This was necessary in order to protect the German forces crossing the Channel.

● RAF pilots, flying Supermarine Spitfire and Hawker Hurricane fighter planes, fought the German air force through the summer of 1940.

● The Germans were defeated not only by the courage of the British pilots but also as a result of mistakes made by the German leadership. The German assault was switched in September from radar stations and air bases to militarily less important targets in London (the *Blitz)*.

Battle of the Atlantic, 1940–43: a British campaign against the German U-boats (submarines) which were sinking merchant ships carrying vital supplies across the Atlantic during the Second World War.

● Germany tried to starve Britain into surrender by depriving it of food and other essential supplies that were being transported from the USA. It was hard for

Britain to protect against this threat since the 'wolf packs' (groups of submarines) were able to operate at will and escape under water.

- Britain eventually defeated the U-boats by developing improved underwater detection methods and by using long-range aircraft which could pursue the enemy in mid-Atlantic.

BBC: see *British Broadcasting Corporation*.

Beaconsfield, Lord: see *Disraeli, Benjamin*.

Beaverbrook, Lord (Max Aitken) (1873–1964): the wealthy owner of the *Daily Express* and a powerful force in *Conservative Party* affairs between the world wars.

- Beaverbrook served in government during both world wars and was a close associate of *Winston Churchill*.
- He was widely distrusted for using his influence behind the scenes. He was an opponent of *Baldwin*, whom he tried to remove as Conservative leader in 1929–31 and again during the *Abdication Crisis* of 1936.
- He campaigned in the press for Empire Free Trade (an updated version of *tariff reform*) and against British membership of the *European Economic Community*.

Bedchamber Crisis, 1839: a constitutional crisis caused by Sir Robert *Peel*'s objection to the holding of posts at Queen *Victoria*'s Court by members of the opposing *Whig Party*.

- In 1839, the Whig Prime Minister, *Melbourne*, was defeated in a vote on the Jamaican constitution and offered his resignation. Victoria invited Peel, the *Conservative Party* leader, to form a government. He asked for the removal of certain ladies from positions at Court because they were related to leading Whig politicians. He regarded this as a crucial test of the Queen's confidence in her new ministers.
- The Queen refused the request and Melbourne, although politically weakened, returned to office. He continued as Prime Minister until defeated in the 1841 general election.
- *TIP* Although apparently trivial, the episode demonstrates the unevenness of Britain's development towards a *constitutional monarchy*. At this early stage in her reign, Queen Victoria ran the risk of identifying the monarchy too closely with one political party.

BEF: see *British Expeditionary Force*.

Benthamism (also known as 'utilitarianism'): the teaching of the philosopher Jeremy Bentham (1748–1832), who argued that government should be judged on its ability to promote 'the greatest happiness of the greatest number'.

- According to Benthanism, institutions must be subject to a test of 'utility', i.e. they must be assessed for their efficiency.
- Benthamite ideas influenced many of the reforms passed by the *Whig* governments of the 1830s. An example was the *New Poor Law* of 1834, which was designed to create an efficiently run, cost-effective and uniform system of workhouses for the relief of poverty.

■ *TIP* Be able to identify the influence of Benthamite ideas on the other reforms of the 1830s.

Bentinck, Lord George (1802–48): a Conservative MP who led the backbench revolt against *Peel* and the repeal of the *Corn Laws* in 1846.

● He was an aristocratic MP who regarded Sir Robert Peel's repeal of the protective duties on corn as a betrayal of the landed classes and of *Conservative Party* principles.

● He was important for the support which he gave to *Disraeli*'s emergence as a leading figure in the Conservative Party.

Berlin, Congress of, 1878: an international conference at which Britain played an important part in upholding the Turkish (Ottoman) empire against the territorial ambitions of Russia.

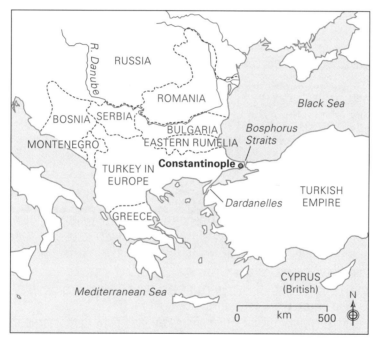

The Balkans after the Congress of Berlin, 1878

● Russia had gone to war with Turkey and imposed the harsh Treaty of San Stefano on the defeated Turks. It proposed the creation of a large Bulgarian state that would be subject to Russian influence.

● This was unacceptable to *Disraeli* as British Prime Minister. He used his influence at Berlin to have the treaty revised. Bulgaria was reduced in size and Britain gained Cyprus as a naval base from Turkey.

■ *TIP* It is important to know about the Congress of Berlin if asked about the *Eastern Question* in the second half of the nineteenth century.

Bevan, Aneurin (1897–1960): Minister of Health 1945–51 under *Attlee* and creator of the *National Health Service* in 1948; Minister of Labour 1951.

b

- Bevan came from a Welsh mining family and earned a reputation before 1945 as a left-wing rebel in the *Labour Party*.
- His proudest achievement was the creation of a system of free health care. He resigned from the Attlee government in protest at health charges imposed by Chancellor *Gaitskell* in his 1951 budget.
- His resignation led to a deep left–right division in the Labour Party. The rift was healed in the late 1950s and Bevan served as deputy leader of the party for a short time before his death.

Beveridge Report, 1942: a wartime report by the civil servant and academic Sir William Beveridge, which proposed a comprehensive system of social insurance for the working population.

- Beveridge identified 'five giants' that must be dealt with: want (poverty), disease, ignorance, squalor and idleness (unemployment).
- He proposed building on the existing *National Insurance* scheme, so that it covered all working people. He also called for government action to guarantee full employment, a *National Health Service* and family allowances (modern child benefit).
- Although many Conservatives questioned the report on grounds of cost, it was generally popular. Its vision of a more just society contributed to the Labour election victory of 1945.
- *TIP* You need to be able to trace the connections between the report and the reforms of the postwar *Attlee* government.

Bevin, Ernest (1881–1951): a leading trade unionist; Minister of Labour and National Service 1940–45; Foreign Secretary 1945–51.

- Bevin was a self-educated manual labourer who rose to prominence in the trade union world as an organiser of the dock workers.
- He was the founder and general secretary (1921–40) of the largest union, the Transport and General Workers' Union.
- As Minister of Labour in the *Churchill coalition*, he was responsible for the mobilisation of the work-force for the war effort.
- As Foreign Secretary in the *Attlee* government, Bevin took a strongly anti-communist line in the *Cold War*. He played an important role in securing US support for western Europe and in the foundation of the *North Atlantic Treaty Organisation (NATO)* in 1949.

Birmingham Political Union (BPU): see *political unions*.

Black and Tans: an irregular volunteer force, recruited by the British government after the First World War to help the police and Army against the Irish republican terrorist movement.

- The name is thought to derive from the dark caps and khaki tunics worn by the volunteers.
- The force earned a reputation for indiscriminate brutality, on a par with the violence of the *IRA*, and thus helped to discredit the *Lloyd George* government's policy towards Irish republicanism.

Black Wednesday, 1992: see *Exchange Rate Mechanism.*

Blair, Tony (1953–): leader of the *Labour Party* since 1994 and Prime Minister since 1997.

- Blair was elected Labour leader following the sudden death of John Smith (leader 1992–94). He imposed a new discipline on the party, re-branded it as 'New Labour' and defeated *Major*'s Conservative government in the 1997 general election.
- 'New Labour' was able to reach beyond the traditional working-class heartlands of the party, to reassure middle-class voters that it had broken with the 'tax and spend' policies of the past.
- In office, Blair has been criticised for allowing media management ('spin') to get out of hand, and it has been suggested that his government lacks ideological coherence and depth.

TIP How far has Blair changed the Labour Party? You should be able to cite examples of continuity and change between 'Old' and 'New' Labour.

Blanketeers: a group of Manchester cotton weavers who tried to march to London in 1817 to protest about deteriorating social and economic conditions.

- The marchers took their name from the blankets in which they draped themselves to draw attention to their protest.
- The background of the episode is the unsympathetic attitude of *Liverpool*'s Tory government towards *Radical* protest.
- The march ended in failure after the authorities at Stockport, Cheshire, reacted in a heavy-handed way.

Blitz: the period of intense German bombing of British cities during the Second World War, from 1940 to 1941.

- The term comes from the German word for 'lightning'. The bombing targeted strategically important areas, such as the London docks, but also caused extensive civilian casualties.
- The experience of the Blitz helped to create a feeling of solidarity among the British population. The sense of shared sacrifice was important in fostering a desire for a fairer society arising out of postwar reconstruction.

Bloody Sunday: (1) clashes between police and unemployed demonstrators in Trafalgar Square, November 1887; (2) the shooting of 14 Irish Catholic civil rights demonstrators by British paratroops in Londonderry (Derry City), January 1972.

- 'Bloody Sunday' in Northern Ireland was important because of the stimulus it gave to Catholic/nationalist support for the *IRA*. As a result, the *Heath* government suspended the Protestant-dominated government of Northern Ireland, based at Stormont, and introduced *direct rule* from Westminster.

Bradlaugh case, 1880–85: a long-running dispute over the right of Charles Bradlaugh, elected as Liberal MP for Northampton, to take his seat in the *House of Commons.*

- Bradlaugh was an atheist whose conscience did not allow him to take the religious oath, which was a requirement for sitting in the House of Commons.

A committee of the Commons decided that he did not have the right to sit. He was returned by his constituents until the House of Commons finally allowed him in.

- The incident caused embarrassment for the *Gladstone* government and for the official leadership of the *Conservative Party*, which failed to make effective use of it. A small group of backbenchers, including *Lord Randolph Churchill* and *Balfour*, became known as the 'Fourth Party' through their persistent exploitation of the case.

Bretton Woods Conference, 1944: an international finance meeting, held in the USA, which created new organisations to promote world trade.

- The conference set up the *International Monetary Fund (IMF)*, to provide countries with a reserve of gold and currency to help them with *balance of payments* problems.
- The World Bank was created to provide loans for development projects.
- Britain gave in to US pressure for *free trade*. The conference led in 1947 to the General Agreement on Tariffs and Trade (GATT), whose purpose was to remove restrictions on international trade. It is now called the World Trade Organisation.

British Broadcasting Corporation (BBC): the main public service radio (and later television) broadcasting organisation in the UK, formed in 1926.

- It was set up as the British Broadcasting Company in 1922 and converted into a public corporation in 1926. This meant that it was run by a board of directors appointed by the government, but it had freedom to manage itself without government interference.
- The most important influence on the early BBC was Sir John Reith (1889–1971), who was Director-General from 1927 to 1938. He insisted that broadcasting was a serious business and that there was a duty to inform and educate as well as entertain.
- The first television broadcasts began in 1936 but were interrupted by the Second World War. Television coverage of Queen Elizabeth II's coronation in 1953 is usually seen as the moment at which television became an important medium in Britain.
- From 1955, the BBC faced competition from Independent Television (ITV).

British empire: the collection of territories which accepted the authority of the British Crown between the eighteenth and late twentieth centuries.

- The North American colonies, which won their independence in 1783, are often described as the 'first British empire'. In the nineteenth century, Britain gained a second empire in Africa and Asia.
- It reached its maximum extent at the end of the First World War, covering one quarter of the world's land area.
- It consisted of a number of different types of territory: self-governing *Dominions* such as Canada, New Zealand and Australia; crown colonies directly ruled by British administrators; and protectorates, where native rulers agreed to govern in co-operation with the imperial power.

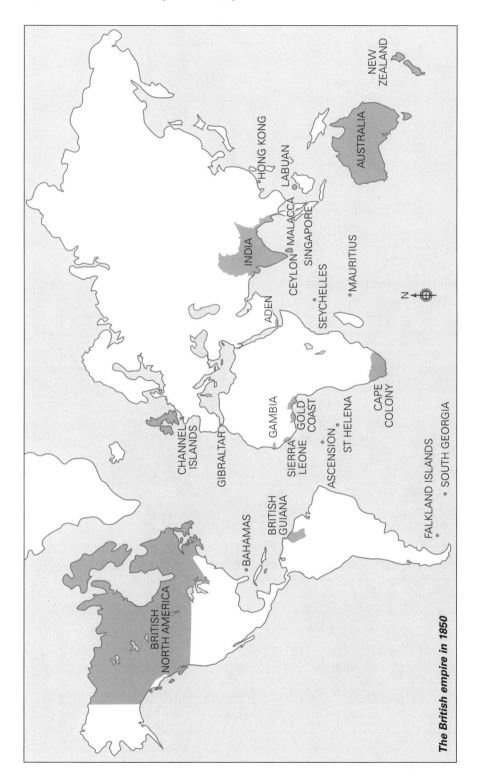

NEW ZEALAND

AUSTRALIA

HONG KONG
LABUAN

MALACCA
CEYLON
SINGAPORE

INDIA

MAURITIUS

SEYCHELLES

ADEN

N

CAPE
COLONY

GAMBIA
GOLD
COAST

SIERRA
LEONE
ASCENSION
ST HELENA

CHANNEL
ISLANDS

GIBRALTAR

FALKLAND ISLANDS
SOUTH GEORGIA

BAHAMAS

BRITISH
GUIANA

BRITISH
NORTH AMERICA

The British empire in 1850

b

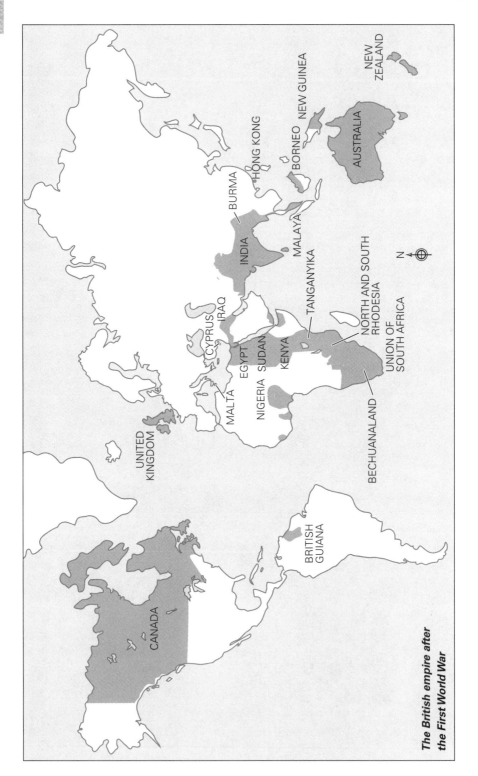

*The British empire after
the First World War*

- The 1931 Statute of Westminster began the empire's gradual transformation into a British Commonwealth, consisting of states linked together in voluntary association with Britain.
- The centre of the empire was India, which gained its independence in 1947. In the following two decades, Britain withdrew from territories in Africa and elsewher e.

British Expeditionary Force (BEF): the military force sent to France on the outbreak of the First World War to stop the German advance to the west.

- The force was created as part of the military reforms of *Haldane* as War Secretary from 1905 to 1912.
- The BEF was known as the 'Old Contemptibles', an ironic allusion to a remark made by Kaiser William II, that it was 'a contemptible little army'.
- It helped to halt the German advance at the battles of Mons and the Marne in August–September 1914. This led the war to settle down into a pattern of trench warfare on the Western Front.

British Union of Fascists: see *Mosley, Sir Oswald*.

Brunel, Isambard Kingdom (1806–59): a leading engineer and entrepreneur of the railway building age.

- Brunel was a gifted engineer who played a major role in the expansion of Britain's rail network in the 1840s and 1850s. His most famous achievement was the building of the Clifton suspension bridge.
- Towards the end of his career, Brunel became involved in steamship design and was responsible for the *Great Eastern*, the *Great Western* and the *Great Britain*.

Bulgarian atrocities, 1876: massacres carried out by the Turks when a rebellion broke out in Bulgaria, part of the Turkish empire.

- The Bulgarian people were Christians who wanted freedom from the Muslim Turkish empire.
- In Britain, news of the massacres created great indignation, especially among Liberals, who accused *Disraeli*'s Conservative government of indifference on a major human rights issue.
- The crusade for justice on behalf of the Bulgarians was led by *Gladstone*, who addressed public meetings and wrote a popular pamphlet, 'The Bulgarian horrors and the question of the East'.

  ▪ *TIP* The episode is a useful illustration of the different priorities of Gladstone and Disraeli in foreign affairs.

Butler, Richard Austen ('Rab') (1902–82): President of the Board of Education 1941–45; Chancellor of the Exchequer 1951–55; a senior figure in Conservative governments up to 1964.

- Butler was the author of the *Education Act, 1944*, which introduced universal secondary education.
- He was a leading force in the revival of the *Conservative Party* after its 1945 election defeat, helping to give it a moderate, progressive image in the period 1951–64.

- He failed to become Prime Minister in January 1957, when *Macmillan* succeeded *Eden*, and again in 1963 when he was beaten by *Douglas-Home*.

Butt, Isaac (1813–79): founder of the Home Government Association in 1870, the body which developed into the *Irish National Party*.

- Butt was a Protestant lawyer who campaigned for Ireland to have its own parliament (*Home Rule*).

- Although his followers won 57 seats in the 1874 general election, he was regarded as too moderate by radical nationalists. He died in 1879. After the brief chairmanship of William Shaw (1879–80) the more aggressive *Parnell* took over leadership of the Irish nationalist movement.

Cabinet: the group of senior government ministers, chaired by the *Prime Minister,* with overall responsibility for policy making.

- The idea of a cohesive group of ministers, which dealt with the monarch as a body, was established by the early nineteenth century. The convention was that a *constitutional monarch* must accept the advice of his or her ministers, or they would resign and the monarch would have to find an alternative group of advisers. This was established during the long premiership of *Liverpool* (1812–27).
- The convention of collective responsibility is crucial to the operation of the Cabinet. All ministers are expected to support an agreed policy position in public. If they disagree, they are expected to resign.
- The Cabinet usually consists of just over 20 members. In wartime, in order to facilitate quick decision making, twentieth-century Prime Ministers have tended to use a smaller War Cabinet of hand-picked ministers.
- After 1945, the growing volume of government business has meant that more decisions are taken by Cabinet committees than by the full Cabinet.

Callaghan, James (1912–): Chancellor of the Exchequer 1964–67; Home Secretary 1967–70; Foreign Secretary 1974–76; Prime Minister 1976–79; leader of the *Labour Party* 1976–80.

- His reputation as Chancellor was damaged when he was forced into *devaluation of the pound* in November 1967, contradicting the Labour government's official position.
- As Prime Minister, he generated a moderate, reassuring image, but faced considerable problems as his parliamentary majority disappeared, leaving him dependent on a deal with the *Liberal Party*.
- A financial crisis in September 1976 forced him to seek a loan from the *International Monetary Fund (IMF)* and to introduce public-spending cuts.
- He lost the 1979 general election to the Conservatives under Margaret *Thatcher*, after the trade unions broke government guidelines on pay in the *'winter of discontent', 1978–79*.

■ *TIP* Callaghan is sometimes seen as a transitional figure between Old Labour and the New Labour Party of *Blair*.

Campaign for Nuclear Disarmament (CND): a pressure group formed in 1958 to work for the abolition of British nuclear weapons, as an encouragement to other countries to do the same.

- The campaign has its origins in the *Cold War*, when there was widespread fear of destruction through nuclear war.
- In the late 1950s and early 1960s, protestors marched on the atomic research base at Aldermaston, Berkshire. In the early 1980s, the organisation was revived when the USA stationed medium-range Cruise missiles at the Greenham Common air base. A group of women camped outside the base for many years.
- Opponents of CND argued that they were too trusting of the Soviet Union and claimed that some members were Soviet sympathisers.

Campbell-Bannerman, Sir Henry (1836–1908): Chief Secretary for Ireland 1884–85; Secretary for War 1886, 1892–95; leader of the *Liberal Party,* 1899–1908; Prime Minister 1905–08.

- As Liberal leader, he inherited a difficult situation, with the party divided between supporters and opponents of the *Anglo–Boer War, 1899–1902*. He managed to restore unity by the time *Balfour*'s Conservative government collapsed in 1905.
- He won a large majority over the Conservatives in the 1906 general election.
- He promoted ministers, such as *Lloyd George* and *Asquith*, who introduced important social reforms, such as *old age pensions*.

Canning, George (1770–1827): Foreign Secretary 1807–09, 1822–27; Prime Minister 1827.

- As Foreign Secretary, he pursued a policy that was generally independent of the continental European powers. His priority was to maintain British prestige and trading interests overseas.
- He had the reputation of favouring liberal constitutional movements to a greater degree than his predecessor and rival, *Castlereagh*. For example, in 1824, he recognised the independence of Spain's former colonies in Latin America. In 1826, he intervened in Portugal to uphold its independence against a royal faction with Spanish connections.
- In domestic politics, he was a *Liberal Tory* who supported *Catholic emancipation*. Right-wing Tories such as *Wellington* refused to serve under him as Prime Minister.

 TIP A common exam question asks you to compare and contrast the foreign policy of Canning and Castlereagh. Ensure that you know the points of continuity as well as change between the two.

Captain Swing riots, 1830–31: a wave of violent protests by agricultural labourers in southern England, caused mainly by rural unemployment.

- The name 'Captain Swing' was a bogus one, used by the protestors when they sent threatening messages to farmers and landowners.
- Labourers destroyed threshing machines, which they blamed for their poverty. The violence alarmed the landowning classes and the government responded with harsh measures.

- The protests strengthened the case made by critics of the parish-based *Old Poor Law*, which was said to be in need of reform. It was argued that the alleged generosity of the system had caused the poor to forget their duty to obey their social superiors.

Cardwell Army reforms: a series of changes introduced by Edward Cardwell, War Secretary 1868–74, to improve the efficiency of the Army and to cut down the privileges of the officer class.

- The reforms were a response to the need for modernisation, indicated by the poor military administration of the *Crimean War* and by the advances made by other powers such as Prussia.
- The reforms cut back expensive overseas garrisons, revised the terms of enlistment and increased the authority of the War Secretary.
- The most controversial aspect was the abolition of the old system whereby officers had bought commissions.
- The reforms still left the Army with considerable organisational weaknesses, as its performance in the *Anglo–Boer War, 1899–1902* was to demonstrate.

Carlton Club revolt, 1922: a meeting of Conservative backbenchers in the party's London headquarters, the Carlton Club, which voted to end membership of the *Lloyd George coalition* government.

- The *Conservative Party* had belonged to the Lloyd George coalition since its formation in 1916. It remained allied to him after the 1918 general election.
- By 1922, many Conservatives had become disillusioned with Lloyd George's tendency to run the government as a one-man band. They disliked the frequent changes of policy and the air of corruption that surrounded the sale of political honours to wealthy backers. By voting at the Carlton Club in October 1922 to fight the next election as an independent party, Conservative MPs paved the way for their domination of interwar politics.
- Keynote speeches at the meeting were made by two leading Conservatives, *Law* and *Baldwin.*

  TIP A knowledge of the proceedings at the Carlton Club is important for exam questions on the decline and fall of Lloyd George.

Caroline, affair of Queen, 1820–21: a political crisis caused by the announcement of the Prince Regent (who became George IV in 1820) of his intention to divorce his wife, Caroline.

- George and Caroline had lived apart for many years and in 1820 he asked the Prime Minister, *Liverpool*, to arrange a divorce. This required the passage of a bill through Parliament.
- Caroline returned to England to demand the title of Queen and her case was taken up by opponents of the Tory government. There were popular demonstrations in her favour. Eventually Caroline was paid off, dying soon afterwards.
- The affair made the government seem out of touch with public opinion and some historians have claimed that it helped to push the Liverpool government in a more *Liberal Tory* direction.

Carson, Sir Edward (1854–1935): Solicitor-General 1900–05; Attorney General 1915; First Lord of the Admiralty 1916–17; Minister without Portfolio 1917–18.

- Carson trained as a lawyer, and was a passionate supporter of the *Act of Union* between Britain and Ireland. He led the Irish Unionists in opposition to the *Asquith* government's 1912 *Home Rule* Bill.
- He played a crucial role in the *Ulster Crisis, 1912–14,* forming the Ulster Volunteer Force in 1913. This organisation made plans for resistance to any attempt to impose Home Rule on Ireland.
- His actions helped to guarantee the place of Ulster in the UK, but he was opposed to the compromise *Anglo–Irish Treaty, 1921* and retired from politics.
- *TIP* Carson is a key figure in the study of Ireland from 1912 to 1921.

Castlereagh, Viscount (Robert Stewart) (1769–1822): Foreign Secretary 1812–22; became Lord Londonderry in 1821.

- Castlereagh was Britain's representative at the Congress of *Vienna* (1814–15), an international gathering to restore European stability after the Napoleonic Wars. His main aim was to ensure that the *balance of power* was not disturbed by a French revival.
- He co-operated with the other European powers in the *congress system* (a series of high-level meetings), but became increasingly detached from them. His 1820 State Paper distanced Britain from the idea of joint intervention in the internal affairs of other countries.
- He was unpopular with *Radicals* in Britain because he was seen as a right-wing Tory in domestic affairs.
- He committed suicide in 1822.
- *TIP* Make sure that you can compare and contrast the foreign policy of Castlereagh and Canning.

Cat and Mouse Act, 1913: the popular name for the 'Prisoners' Temporary Discharge for Ill Health Act', passed by the *Asquith* government to cope with the problems caused when members of the *Women's Social and Political Union (WSPU)* went on hunger strike in prison.

- Many campaigners for female votes, after being sent to prison for violent acts, refused to eat and had to be forcibly fed. This caused embarrassment to the Liberal government.
- The act allowed prison authorities to release women who became ill while on hunger strike. They could be rearrested when their health had recovered. This was widely seen as unfair and worsened the government's public relations problems.

Catholic emancipation: the right of Catholics to sit as MPs, which was conceded in 1829.

- Roman Catholics were traditionally denied equal political rights with members of the Church of England. Fear of Catholic influence dated back to the religious conflicts of the sixteenth century. Protestants were suspicious of Catholics because it was believed that they placed their loyalty to the Pope above their loyalty to the British Crown.

- Catholic emancipation was a live political issue in the early nineteenth century. Pro-emancipation *Liberal Tories* like *Canning* disagreed with their more right-wing colleagues.
- The issue was forced in 1829 when the Irish leader, *O'Connell*, won a seat in a by-election. *Wellington*'s government granted emancipation out of fear of civil war in Ireland, causing a deep rift in the *Tory Party*. It was seen as a serious betrayal by the anti-Catholic *Ultras.*
- **TIP** Catholic emancipation is important in the disintegration of the Tory Party and in the emergence of *parliamentary reform* as a major issue in the early 1830s.

Cato Street conspiracy, 1820: a plot to assassinate the members of the *Liverpool Cabinet,* which was frustrated by the action of a government spy.

- The plotters, led by Arthur Thistlewood, wanted a people's uprising against the Tory government. They were arrested while meeting in a house in Cato Street, London.
- The conspiracy underlined the unpopularity of the government with *Radicals,* who wanted more rights for the mass of the population.
- **TIP** Some historians have used the conspiracy to illustrate the so-called 'repressive phase' of the Liverpool government, which ended in the years 1820–22.

Chadwick, Edwin (1800–90): a social investigator and reformer; secretary to the Poor Law Commission 1832–46; author of the 1842 'Report on the Sanitary Condition of the Labouring Poor'.

- Chadwick was heavily influenced by the ideas of *Benthamism,* and believed in efficient central government.
- He was the driving force behind the *New Poor Law, 1834*. He wanted to see a cheaply administered, centrally supervised, uniform system of poor relief. The new arrangements did not completely meet his expectations in practice, although he defended the New Poor Law against its critics.
- His 1842 report on urban sanitary problems influenced the *Public Health Act, 1848*. However, he would have preferred the act to have had more compulsory features.

Chamberlain, Austen (1863–1937): Chancellor of the Exchequer 1903–05, 1919–21; India Secretary 1915–17; leader of the *Conservative Party* 1921–22; Foreign Secretary 1924–29.

- He was the son of *Joseph Chamberlain* and the half-brother of *Neville Chamberlain.*
- As Conservative leader, he was a failure because his support for the *Lloyd George coalition* was out of step with rank-and-file opinion in his own party. He spent some time in the political wilderness after the *Carlton Club revolt.*
- As Foreign Secretary, he aimed to stabilise Europe by healing the divisions between France and Germany after the First World War.

- His main achievement was the 1925 Locarno Pact, under which Germany agreed to respect its borders with France and Belgium.

Chamberlain, Joseph (1836–1914): President of the Board of Trade 1880–85; President of the Local Government Board 1886; Colonial Secretary 1895–1903.

- He made his reputation as a reforming Mayor of Birmingham, serving as Birmingham MP from 1876.
- Originally, he was a radical member of the *Liberal Party*, who built the first professional party organisation in British politics.
- He broke with the Liberals in opposition to *Home Rule* for Ireland, and ended his career as an ally of the Conservatives and a keen supporter of empire.
- He divided the Conservatives in 1903 with his proposals for *tariff reform*, contributing to their heavy election defeat in 1906.

TIP Chamberlain's destructive impact on two political parties is a common exam question theme.

Chamberlain, Neville (1869–1940): Chancellor of the Exchequer 1923–24, 1931–37; Minister of Health 1922–23, 1924–29; Prime Minister and leader of the *Conservative Party* 1937–40.

- As Health Minister, he introduced a number of social reforms, including contributory pensions and allowances for widows and orphans.
- As Prime Minister, he is mainly associated with the *appeasement* of Hitler's Germany. He secured the *Munich Agreement* on the future of Czechoslovakia in September 1938 but went reluctantly to war with Germany a year later.
- He was ineffective as a war leader and was replaced by *Winston Churchill* in May 1940, following failure of the expedition against the German occupation of Norway.

Chanak Crisis, 1922: a crisis in which Britain almost went to war with Turkey. It helped to bring down the *Lloyd George coalition* government.

- After the First World War, British troops formed part of an Allied force safeguarding the Dardanelles (the narrow strip of water between Europe and Asia, linking the Black Sea and the Mediterranean).
- In September 1922, a Turkish army was engaged in reconquering the area, which had been occupied by Greece under the terms of the *Paris Peace Conference, 1919*. The other members of the Allied force withdrew, but Lloyd George ordered the British garrison at Chanak, on the eastern side of the Dardanelles, to stand firm.
- The dispute was settled by the local commanders without fighting, but Lloyd George's apparent willingness to risk a war encouraged many Conservatives to bring down his government in the October 1922 *Carlton Club revolt*.

Chartism: the first large-scale working-class movement in Britain, which aimed to improve conditions for the poor by seeking an extension of democracy.

- Chartists were disappointed by the failure of the 1832 *Franchise Act* to extend the vote to working-class people. They were also motivated by anger over unemployment and the harshness of the *New Poor Law, 1834*.

- They presented three mass petitions to Parliament, in 1839, 1842 and 1848, calling for acceptance of the 'People's Charter'.
- Their main demands were for manhood suffrage (the extension of the vote to all men over 21), the *secret ballot* and annual parliaments. They also wanted MPs to be paid, to represent constituencies (areas) of equal size and to be allowed to sit in Parliament regardless of their personal property. Although Parliament rejected the petitions, all of these demands (except for annual parliaments) were eventually granted.
- Chartism was weakened by divisions over methods. 'Moral force' Chartists such as William Lovett (1800–77) insisted on peaceful protest and links with middle-class sympathisers. 'Physical force' Chartists such as Feargus *O'Connor* believed in using force or the threat of force against the authorities, as in the *Newport Rising, 1839.*

■ *TIP* For questions on Chartism, you need to be able to analyse the reasons for its growth and for its ultimate failure.

Chinese slavery: a label applied by opponents of *Balfour*'s Conservative government in 1903–06, to describe the importation of cheap Chinese labour into South Africa.

- At the end of the *Anglo–Boer War, 1899–1902,* the British government had to find ways of reviving the South African economy. The High Commissioner in Cape Colony, *Milner,* authorised the importation of cheap Chinese labour to run the gold mines.
- Liberal opponents of the government condemned the immorality of herding labourers into camps with few rights. Trade unionists were also worried that the Conservatives might use similar methods in Britain to undercut white workers, as the Chinese would work for very low wages. This helped to lose the Conservatives the working-class vote in the 1906 general election.

Churchill, Lord Randolph (1849–95): India Secretary 1885–86; Chancellor of the Exchequer 1886.

- Lord Churchill was an aristocratic Conservative MP who reached *Cabinet* rank by challenging the party leadership in the early 1880s.
- He popularised the idea of 'Tory Democracy' — an ill-defined claim that the *Conservative Party* was most in tune with the working classes.
- He ruined his career by an ill-judged resignation as Chancellor from the *Salisbury* government in December 1886.
- He was the father of *Winston Churchill.*

Churchill, Sir Winston (1874–1965): President of the Board of Trade 1908–10; Home Secretary 1910–11; First Lord of the Admiralty 1911–15, 1939–40; Minister of Munitions 1917–18; War Secretary 1918–21; Colonial Secretary 1921–22; Chancellor of the Exchequer 1924–29; Prime Minister 1940–45, 1951–55; leader of the *Conservative Party* 1940–55.

- Winston Churchill was elected as a Conservative MP in 1900, became a Liberal in 1904 and returned to the Conservatives in 1924.

- His aggressive attitude to trade union unrest before the First World War and to the 1926 *General Strike* made him unpopular with the Labour movement.
- He spent the 1930s in political isolation as an opponent of the *National Government* policy of extending self-government to India. He later called for more extensive rearmament against the threat of Nazi Germany.
- He was an inspirational war leader from 1940 to 1945, unequalled for his ability to rally public support through his speeches and for his energetic organisation of the war effort.
- He was defeated by *Attlee*'s *Labour Party* in the 1945 general election but returned to power in the 1951 election.

Church of England: see *Anglican Church*.

Citizen's Charter, 1991: an initiative launched by the *Major* government to make public servants more answerable to the public and to improve the standards of service provided.

- The charter affected civil servants who deal with the public — for example those who deal with passports, or with claims for social security benefits.
- Targets were set for the speed of civil servants' response to members of the public, and 'Charter Marks' were awarded for high-quality service.
- The Labour government accepted the basic idea behind the charter. In 1998 it created the 'Service First' programme to monitor the quality of services.

Clause Four: the best-known part of the *Labour Party*'s 1918 Constitution, which committed it to achieving the nationalisation (state ownership) of the main industries and services.

- Clause Four became the essential definition of the Labour Party's goals for most of the twentieth century. The *Attlee* governments of 1945–51 carried out an extensive programme of nationalisation.
- In the 1950s, Labour Party members could not agree on whether to continue with further nationalisation or to consolidate earlier achievements and concentrate instead on promoting equality through social reforms.
- In 1995, *Blair* persuaded the party to accept a new, looser rewriting of Clause Four that moved away from the idea of state control of the economy.

▥ *TIP* In questions on changing Labour Party policies, be sure to define nationalisation clearly.

CND: see *Campaign for Nuclear Disarmament*.

coalition: a government that contains representatives of more than one party; in British politics, coalitions have usually arisen because of war or some other national emergency.

- The *Asquith* government of 1915–16 and the *Churchill* government of 1940–45 were all-party coalitions of Conservatives, Labour and Liberals.
- Other governments, although known as coalitions, did not include all the main parties. The Conservatives did not take part in the *Aberdeen* government of 1852–55. Not all Liberals joined the *Lloyd George* coalition in 1916, and Labour members left it at the end of the First World War. The *National Governments* of

C

1931–40 were dominated by the Conservatives, who combined with ex-Liberal MPs (known as *Liberal Nationals*) and ex-Labour MPs (known as National Labour).

▨ *TIP* Distinguish between full coalitions and arrangements where a party gives its support to a government without actually joining it. An example of the latter is the *Lib–Lab Pact* of 1977–78, when the *Liberal Party* kept *Callaghan*'s Labour government in office.

Cobden, Richard (1819–65): a *Radical* Liberal MP who led the campaign against the *Corn Laws* and was the main advocate of a peaceful, non-interventionist foreign policy in mid-Victorian Britain.

● Cobden organised the *Anti-Corn Law League* with John Bright (1811–89).
● He gave his name to 'Cobdenism', the idea that nations should neither spend large sums on defence nor pursue active, aggressive foreign policies. This approach was also known as the 'Manchester School', after the centre of *free trade* support.
● He believed that free trade would help to promote peace as well as prosperity, and negotiated the 1860 Anglo–French trade treaty, which reduced the taxes paid by French and British merchants when they exported goods to each other.

Coercion Acts: exceptional measures taken by British governments to uphold public order in nineteenth-century Ireland.

● The acts gave governments emergency powers to arrest and detain individuals suspected of being hostile to British authority.
● Liberal governments, such as that of *Gladstone* in 1881, resorted to coercion with reluctance because it interfered with personal freedom.
● Measures of coercion were often accompanied by moderate reforms — measures of 'conciliation' designed to win over the Irish people. For example, in 1881 an *Irish Land Act* was also introduced.

Cold War, 1945–91: a period of international tension between the USA and its allies and the communist USSR and its allies.

● The Cold War involved conflict that stopped short of war but included spying, economic warfare, propaganda and a build-up of military forces, including nuclear weaponry.
● Britain was involved through its support for the USA, upon whom it was dependent for its economic recovery after the Second World War. It also developed its own nuclear weapons and allowed the USA to base bomber aircraft and missiles on its territory.
● Britain supported the USA in several major international crises. For example, it sent troops as part of a US-led force to participate in the Korean War (1950–53), when communist North Korea invaded non-communist South Korea.

Collins, Michael: see *Irish Republican Army (IRA)*.

Combination Acts, 1799–1800: laws passed by *Pitt*'s government, which made trade unions illegal.

- Trade unions were defined as 'combinations' of working men 'in restraint of trade'. Their banning was a response to fear of *Radical* organisation at the time of the *French Revolution*.
- The ban was lifted in 1824 following a report by a Select Committee of the House of Commons, dominated by Radicals.

Common Market: see *European Economic Community.*

Commonwealth, British: see *British empire.*

Common Wealth Party: an idealistic left-wing political party, founded in 1942 by the former Liberal MP Sir Richard Acland.

- During the Second World War, as a mark of their commitment to national unity, the main political parties agreed not to contest by-elections. Common Wealth was founded by a group of people who wanted to register their opposition to *Churchill*'s government and to the *Conservative Party*. In normal circumstances, most would have voted Labour.
- Common Wealth stood for the use of property in the interests of the community as a whole. For example, Acland, a large landowner in Devon, handed over his estate to the National Trust.
- The party won three by-elections (all from the Conservatives) and one seat at the 1945 general election before dissolving as normal political life resumed.
- **TIP** Common Wealth is an indicator of the shift of public opinion to the left during the Second World War, which led to the Labour election victory of 1945.

communism: the belief, associated with the nineteenth-century German thinker Karl Marx, that all property should be held in common. Communists looked to a revolution to bring about complete equality in society.

- Fear of communism was an important influence on the thinking of the propertied classes from the end of the First World War. Russian Communists had taken over in 1917 through the violent overthrow of existing authority and had created the world's first 'workers' state'. Under Lenin and Stalin they destroyed democracy and ruled through a one-party state.
- Moderate *Labour Party* and trade union leaders such as *Bevin* were no less fearful of communist influence than the Conservatives were. During *Attlee*'s leadership, several individuals who favoured an alliance with the Communists were expelled from the Labour Party.
- After 1945, the emergence of Soviet Russia as a superpower meant that Britain took the side of the USA in the *Cold War.*
- The Communist Party of Great Britain, formed in 1920, never had a large following and few of its candidates were elected to Parliament.

community charge (also known as 'poll tax'): a way of financing local government, introduced by the *Thatcher* government in 1989–90, which was scrapped 2 years later because of its unpopularity.

- For centuries, local authorities had raised money from a property tax known as the rates. This was linked to the size and standard of the property and not to the number of occupants or the use they made of local authority services.

- The Conservatives introduced the community charge, which was based on residence. The idea was that almost every adult would pay something towards the cost of local services.
- The new tax proved unpopular, because it was unrelated to income and impossible to collect. It was a cause of Thatcher's downfall. The *Major* government replaced it with the council tax, which takes into account both the size of a property and the number of occupants.

congress system: the name given to a series of meetings held after the *Napoleonic Wars,* involving high-level representatives of the *Great Powers.*

- Britain's Foreign Secretary, *Castlereagh*, played a part in setting up the Congress of *Vienna* in 1814–15. The purpose was to settle future disputes by discussion and to restore stability to Europe after the upheavals following the *French Revolution.*
- Congresses were also held at Aix-la-Chapelle (1818), Troppau (1820), Laibach (1821), Verona (1822) and St Petersburg (1825).
- Britain was increasingly uneasy about the use that the continental monarchies of Austria, Prussia and Russia wished to make of the congresses. These powers saw the meetings as a means of organising joint action to suppress movements for change in other countries. Britain did not wish to participate in this kind of interference in other countries' internal affairs.

■ *TIP* The congress system is an important topic in exam questions on the foreign policy of Castlereagh and *Canning.*

conscription: compulsory military service, normally associated in Britain with extreme national need in time of war.

- Conscription was in force in the later part of the First World War, from 1916 to 1918. Its introduction caused problems for the *Liberal Party*, many of whose members viewed it as an inexcusable interference with individual liberty.
- It was also in force throughout the Second World War and was continued until 1960. This was because Britain was trying to keep control of its empire and was supporting the USA in the *Cold War.*
- The 1957 Defence White Paper, a policy statement by Conservative Defence Secretary Duncan Sandys, signalled a scaling down of conventional armed forces and greater reliance on nuclear weapons. It was no longer considered necessary to maintain conscription ('national service') in peacetime.

Conservative Party: a political organisation that evolved in the nineteenth century from the older *Tory Party*, standing for the defence of property and historic institutions, and for resistance to radical change, whether proposed by Liberals or by Labour opponents.

- The starting-point for Conservative thinking is that change is justified only when seen to be a practical necessity. Conservatives stress rights and responsibilities grounded in traditional practice. They have stood for institutions such as the monarchy, Anglicanism and the *British empire* and for the maintenance of social stability.

- Conservatives have generally believed in free enterprise and have distrusted *Labour Party* ideas of socialist planning. This has generally been qualified by an acceptance of the need for moderate social reform, if only to prevent the voters from turning to their opponents.
- The foundation of the party is often dated to the *Tamworth Manifesto* of Sir Robert *Peel* in 1834. Other historians regard *Disraeli* as the real founder of the party.
- The twentieth century has been described as the 'Conservative century', with long periods of dominance by the party — for much of the interwar period, from 1951 to 1964, and from 1979 to 1997.

Conspiracy and Protection of Property Act, 1875: a law passed by *Disraeli*'s government, defining the status and rights of trade unions.

- The act protected unions from prosecution for conspiracy and legalised peaceful picketing — the practice of persuading one's fellow workers not to work during a strike.
- It was accompanied by the Employers and Workmen Act (1875), which placed employers and workers on the same legal footing with regard to the contracts between them.
- This was not final settlement of trade union rights. It was still possiblefor law courts to challenge the right to picket, as in *Lyons v. Wilkins, 1899*.

constitutional monarchy: the idea that a king or queen's power should be limited by a framework of law and custom, so that he or she plays a largely non-political role.

- In Britain, the transformation of the monarchy into a constitutional one was a gradual process. It could be said to have been completed by the end of the reign of Queen *Victoria* (1837–1901).
- Nineteenth-century monarchs possessed considerable powers in theory, but wider political changes meant that these had to be exercised with care, or not at all. William IV (1830–37) was the last monarch to dismiss a government — that of *Melbourne* in 1834 — but the experiment failed because his successor, *Peel,* could not command a majority in the *House of Commons.*
- The slow movement of Britain towards democracy, through a series of *Franchise Acts,* together with the growth of organised political parties, have reduced the monarch's scope for effective involvement in politics.
- The main functions of a constitutional monarch are to represent the nation on ceremonial occasions, to provide a focus for national unity and to be a recognisable symbol of continuity. Influence is usually exercised behind the scenes. This is in accordance with the nineteenth-century writer Walter Bagehot's declaration in 1867 that a constitutional monarch has 'the right to be consulted, the right to encourage and the right to warn'.

Corn Laws, 1815–46: measures introduced to protect the economic position of British landowners and farmers by excluding foreign wheat from the country until British corn had reached a stated price.

- The Corn Laws were modified in 1828 by the introduction of a sliding scale, which increased the duty (tax) on foreign corn if the price of British corn began to fall.

- Even in this form, the laws were very unpopular with consumers, who had to pay artificially high prices for bread, and with manufacturers, who favoured *free trade*.
- The Corn Laws were repealed (abolished) in June 1846 by *Peel*'s government. The action split the *Conservative Party* since it had traditionally stood for the protection of the landowning classes.

■ *TIP* The Corn Laws were a key issue in the politics of 1815–46.

Corrupt and Illegal Practices Act, 1883: an attempt by *Gladstone*'s second government to restrict corruption at elections.

- In spite of the introduction of the secret *ballot* in 1872, there was evidence of continuing corruption in some parliamentary seats.
- The act set strict limits on the amount that candidates could spend in trying to get themselves elected. It imposed penalties for bribery and intimidation of voters.

■ *TIP* The act was an important step in the development of parliamentary democracy in Britain.

County Councils Act, 1888: the creation of a system of councils, elected by ratepayers, that were responsible for local government in the counties of England and Wales.

- The act, passed during *Salisbury*'s Conservative government, transferred responsibility for local government away from the magistrates, who had traditionally administered the counties through their courts.
- It created the first authority to cover the whole of the capital, the London County Council.

Coupon Election, 1918: the name given (by *Asquith*, the Liberal leader) to the general election held in December 1918, after the end of the First World War, which confirmed the *Lloyd George coalition* in office.

- The 'coupon' was the name given to the letter of support sent by Lloyd George and his coalition partner, *Conservative Party* leader Bonar *Law*, to parliamentary candidates of whom they approved.
- The election was fought in an atmosphere of patriotic and anti-German feeling and favoured candidates who had been strongly in favour of fighting the war.
- It hardened the division in the *Liberal Party* between followers of Asquith and Lloyd George, which had developed since the latter took over as Prime Minister in 1916.

Crimean War, 1854–56: a war in which Britain and France fought Russia in order to prevent Russia from expanding into the Turkish empire.

- The Crimean War was an important episode in the *Eastern Question*. It began when Britain and France reacted against Russia's occupation of the Turkish provinces of Moldavia and Wallachia (modern Romania) and its destruction of the Turkish fleet at Sinope on the Black Sea.

C

- The main theatre of war was the Crimean peninsula, in southern Russia, where the objective of the British and French forces was to capture the naval base of Sebastopol.
- Although the Russians were eventually defeated, the war demonstrated the weaknesses of British military administration, the result of many years of economising and neglect.
- The war ended with the Treaty of *Paris*, 1856.

Crystal Palace: an enormous structure of iron and glass, built to house the Great Exhibition of 1851.

- The exhibition was intended to act as a showcase for Britain's achievements as the world's leading industrial power and the centre of a world-wide empire.
- The palace was erected in Hyde Park. After the exhibition was over, the building was taken down and re-sited at Sydenham in south London. It burnt down in an unexplained fire in 1936.

Curragh mutiny, 1914: an episode in March 1914 when a group of British Army officers defied the Liberal government of *Asquith*, which aimed to introduce *Home Rule* for Ireland.

- The incident was not technically a mutiny, since the officers did not disobey an actual order. Nonetheless, it cast serious doubt on the reliability of the Army in Ireland. It was sparked by the news that the Asquith government was preparing to move troops to the north of Ireland, to protect arms supplies.

C

- The background to the incident was the growing hostility of the *Ulster* people to the prospect of Home Rule.
- Many British officers had family backgrounds in Ulster. They learned that the War Secretary, Colonel Seely, was prepared to excuse any officer with a home in Ulster from duty. General Gough and 57 cavalry officers told the Commander-in-Chief in Ireland, General Paget, that they would resign rather than be a party to the use of force against their fellow Ulstermen.
- Seely was forced to resign and his post was temporarily taken over by Asquith. The episode severely damaged the image of the government, which had more or less admitted that it could not impose its Home Rule policy.

▨ *TIP* The Curragh mutiny is important for a study of the *Ulster Crisis* of 1912–14.

decolonisation: the process by which colonies are transformed into independent countries. This happened to the *British empire* between the late 1940s and the 1960s.

- The first territory to become independent was India, which was divided into two new states, India and Pakistan, in 1947. Britain's African colonies received their independence between the mid-1950s and the mid-1960s.
- The rise of nationalist movements, sometimes involving terrorism (e.g. the Mau Mau disturbances in Kenya in the 1950s), played a part in the process of decolonisation.
- After the Second World War, Britain could not sustain the economic burden of empire. Some historians argue that the *Suez Crisis* of 1956 and the withdrawal of other European powers from Africa accelerated the process, by demonstrating to British leaders that they could not hold out against wider changes in the world.
- The transformation of *Rhodesia* into independent Zimbabwe in 1980 is sometimes seen as the last act in the process of decolonisation.
- ▒ *TIP* You need to be familiar with the debates among historians about the various factors leading to decolonisation. Why did the process accelerate so rapidly in the late 1950s/early 1960s?

Derby, Edward Stanley, 14th Earl of (1799–1869): Chief Secretary for Ireland 1830–33; Colonial Secretary 1833–34, 1841–45; Prime Minister 1852, 1858–59, 1866–68; *Conservative Party* leader 1846–68.

- Derby began his career as a *Whig* but moved over to the Conservatives in 1834.
- He broke with *Peel* in 1845–46 because he could not accept the repeal of the *Corn Laws*.
- He led three minority Conservative governments, and was author of the *Franchise Act, 1867*.
- He fostered the career of *Disraeli*, who succeeded him as party leader.
- ▒ *TIP* Do not confuse the 14th Earl with his son, the 15th Earl, who served as Conservative Foreign Secretary 1874–78, then moved over to the Liberals, ending his career as a *Liberal Unionist*.

de Valera, Eamon (1882–1975): Prime Minister of the Irish Free State/Eire/Irish

Republic 1932–48, 1951–55, 1957–59; President of the Irish Republic 1959–73.

- De Valera was an Irish republican leader of Spanish/Irish American parentage. His objective was to create a united Ireland — Catholic and traditional in culture, and independent of Britain.
- He took part in the 1916 *Easter Rising*, escaping execution by the British because of his US citizenship.
- He was President of the illegal republican assembly (the Dáil), formed in 1919 in defiance of British rule. He rejected the *Anglo–Irish Treaty, 1921*, which he saw as an unsatisfactory compromise.
- In 1926, De Valera founded the Fianna Fáil Party, which became the largest party in Southern Ireland.
- He was author of the 1937 constitution, which removed all references to the British Crown and gave a special position to the Catholic Church in the life of the country.

■ *TIP* De Valera was a key figure in the development of an independent Ireland with its own distinctive identity.

devaluation of the pound: a decision to lower the value of the pound in relation to other currencies.

- The value of the pound was fixed at £1:$4.86 in 1925, when Britain returned to the *gold standard*. This was too high a value and meant that British goods were overpriced for export.
- The pound was devalued by the *Attlee* government in 1949. It was then worth $2.80. After a further devaluation, by the *Wilson* government in 1967, it fell to $2.40.
- Devaluation has the effect of making British exports cheaper and thus helps British industry. In both cases, however, government ministers hesitated before taking the decision, partly because it would be seen as damaging to Britain's prestige abroad.

devolution: the transfer of power over a particular area from central government to a regional assembly or parliament.

- Devolution became a political issue after the 1974 general elections, when Scottish and Welsh nationalist parties gained increased representation at Westminster. *Callaghan*'s Labour government held referendums on Scottish and Welsh devolution in 1979, but these failed to achieve the majority of votes necessary.
- During the Conservative governments of 1979–97, there was no progress on devolution. There was an increasing feeling, especially in Scotland, that these areas were not receiving proper treatment. For example, the unpopular *community charge* was tried out first in Scotland.
- After the election of a Labour government in 1997, referendums were held, leading to the establishment of a Welsh assembly in Cardiff and a Scottish parliament, with tax-raising powers, in Edinburgh. The *Good Friday Agreement* of 1998 also created a devolved assembly for Northern Ireland.

Diplock courts: special law courts used in Northern Ireland since 1973, where cases involving terrorist suspects are tried without a jury.

- The courts were recommended in a report made by the judge Lord Diplock. The reason was that in the circumstances of Northern Ireland, it was likely that jury members would be intimidated by paramilitary groups.
- A further report in 2000 recommended that the situation had not yet improved sufficiently to allow the abolition of Diplock courts.

direct rule: in Northern Ireland politics, it refers to the decision by the *Heath* government to suspend the Stormont assembly in 1972.

- Since 1921, Northern Ireland had been ruled by an assembly based at Stormont, a suburb of Belfast. This assembly was dominated by Protestants, and the *Ulster Unionist Party* was the main political party.
- In 1968–69, protests by the Catholic community, demanding equal civil rights with Protestants, led to an outbreak of violence in Northern Ireland. The British government tried to keep order with the use of the Army and police, but *Bloody Sunday* in January 1972 wrecked Catholic and Nationalist confidence in this strategy. As a result, the Heath government decided to suspend the Stormont assembly.
- A new *Cabinet* post, that of Northern Ireland Secretary, was created and Northern Ireland was ruled directly from London. This continued until the *Good Friday Agreement, 1998* opened the prospect of a new assembly for the province.

disestablishment: see *Anglican Church.*

Disraeli, Benjamin (Lord Beaconsfield) (1804–81): Chancellor of the Exchequer 1852, 1858–59, 1866–68; Prime Minister 1868, 1874–80; *Conservative Party* leader in the *House of Commons* from 1849 and overall leader from 1868.

- A Jewish novelist and dandy who was viewed with suspicion on his arrival in the House of Commons in 1837. (At the time there was some anti-Semitic prejudice in upper-class circles.)
- He came to lead the backbench (not holding government office), landowning Conservative MPs after opposing *Peel*'s repeal of the *Corn Laws* in 1846.
- He made the Conservatives once again a viable party of government after guiding the *Franchise Act, 1867* through the House of Commons.
- He passed a number of social reforms, including the *Artisans' Dwellings Act, 1875* and laws on trade unions.
- As Prime Minister, Disraeli identified the Conservatives with the *British empire* by pursuing an energetic anti-Russian policy, purchasing Britain's shares in the Suez Canal and having Queen *Victoria* made Empress of India.
- He lost the 1880 general election to *Gladstone*'s *Liberal Party.*

▓ *TIP* Be able to discuss Disraeli's contribution to the Conservative Party's fortunes — to its failure to secure office for much of the period 1846–66, and to its later revival.

Ditchers: see *Hedgers and Ditchers.*

Dominions: self-governing areas of the *British empire*, the principal ones being

Canada, Australia, New Zealand and South Africa.

● Dominions, which were ruled by white populations, had internal self-government before the First World War.

● They were connected to Britain by economic, historic and emotional ties, but greatly valued their right to run their own affairs.

● The 1931 Statute of Westminster gave them virtual independence. They remained linked to Britain through a common head of state, the British monarch. They formed the nucleus of the British Commonwealth.

▨ *TIP* In questions on the British empire, distinguish between Dominions and colonies, which were ruled directly by British officials.

Don Pacifico affair, 1850: see *Palmerston.*

Douglas-Home, Sir Alec (Lord Home) (1903–95): Foreign Secretary 1960–63, 1970–74; Prime Minister 1963–64; leader of the *Conservative Party* 1963–65.

● Douglas-Home was chosen as Prime Minister in October 1963 following the sudden illness of *Macmillan*. The fact that he came from the *House of Lords* enabled *Wilson*'s *Labour Party* to portray him as out of date and out of touch.

● He narrowly lost the 1964 general election.

● Critics claimed that Douglas-Home had gained the party leadership through the influence of a 'magic circle' of upper-class Conservatives. From 1965, the party adopted an open leadership election process.

Downing Street declaration, 1993: a joint statement by the British and Irish governments that a united Ireland was possible if supported by a majority in both north and south.

● Britain was represented by Prime Minister *Major*, and the Irish Republic by Albert Reynolds.

● The agreement was a response to continuing *IRA* violence and to US pressure for a settlement of the Northern Ireland problem.

● For the first time, Britain publicly declared that it had no selfish strategic or economic interest in Northern Ireland.

● The declaration led to an IRA cease-fire in 1994, but no progress could be made on the decommissioning (putting out of action) of terrorist weapons and the cease-fire ended in 1996.

Dreadnought: a type of 'all big gun' battleship, launched by Britain in 1906, which outclassed the battle fleets of other countries in terms of armour, speed and weaponry.

● The building of the Dreadnoughts was a response to the growth of Germany's battle fleet and led to a race between the two countries for dominance at sea.

● It was part of a programme of naval modernisation led by Sir John Fisher, the First Sea Lord (the most senior admiral) from 1904 to 1910.

● The Dreadnought building programme was accelerated in 1908 after the failure of a disarmament conference at The Hague in Holland.

● The naval race contributed to poor Anglo–German relations prior to the First World War.

Eastern Question: a problem in foreign affairs throughout the nineteenth century, caused by the belief that the Turkish (Ottoman) empire was likely to collapse.

- At the beginning of the nineteenth century, Turkey ruled over a large part of southeastern Europe (the Balkans). Its empire bordered on the narrow stretches of water linking the Black Sea and the Mediterranean (the Straits of the Bosphorus and the Dardanelles).
- European powers disliked the corruption and brutality of the Turkish empire, but realised that its collapse might lead to war between them.
- Britain was particularly concerned to prop up the Turkish empire because it feared that Russia might exploit Turkish weakness in order to extend its power into the region. Russia was viewed as a threat to Britain's naval presence in the Mediterranean and to its Indian empire.
- The Eastern Question was at the centre of several episodes involving Britain, including the *Crimean War, 1854–56* and the events leading up to the Congress of *Berlin* in 1878.

■ *TIP* In answering questions on this topic, remember to analyse why Britain was involved, rather than simply describing events.

Easter Rising, 1916: a rebellion against British rule in Ireland, carried out by the Irish Republican Brotherhood (IRB).

- The IRB were not satisfied with *Home Rule* for Ireland; they wanted total independence from Britain and the creation of an Irish republic.
- They used Britain's wartime difficulties as an opportunity to launch an armed uprising in Dublin. They captured the General Post Office and other buildings, but were suppressed by British troops.
- The rising itself commanded little support, but the ferocity of the British response — 16 captured rebels were executed — turned southern Irish opinion in favour of the republican movement.

■ *TIP* A knowledge of the Easter Rising is crucial for an understanding of the events leading to the *Anglo–Irish Treaty, 1921*.

Ecclesiastical Titles Act, 1851: an attempt by *Russell's Whig* government to ban the Roman Catholic Church from adopting territorial titles for its bishops, such as 'Archbishop of Westminster'.

- The act was a response to the so-called 'Papal aggression' — a decision by the Catholic Church to divide Britain up for administrative purposes into dioceses (areas presided over by bishops). The organisation of the Catholic Church had been semi-underground since the creation of the Church of England in the sixteenth century.
- The act was a bid for popularity by the Russell government, which saw that the Catholic Church's move had sparked a wave of Protestant opposition.
- It was later seen as an example of indefensible religious prejudice and was repealed by *Gladstone*'s first government.
- ■ *TIP* The act demonstrates that the Whigs' commitment to religious toleration was stronger in the case of Protestant *nonconformists* than of Roman Catholics.

Eden, Sir Anthony (Lord Avon) (1897–1977): Foreign Secretary 1935–38, 1940–45, 1951–55; Prime Minister and leader of the *Conservative Party* 1955–57.

- Eden was a moderate Conservative in home affairs, who popularised the idea of a 'property-owning democracy'.
- His experience was mainly in foreign affairs. In the 1930s, he made a name as a young, attractive minister, a champion of collective security through the *League of Nations*. He resigned from *Neville Chamberlain*'s government over the Prime Minister's dealings with Italian dictator Mussolini.
- His career was restored by his association with Chamberlain's successor, *Winston Churchill*, whom he served as Foreign Secretary. Eden was seen as Churchill's heir but had to wait until 1955 for the opportunity to succeed him.
- Eden's career was destroyed by his decision to attack Egypt in the *Suez Crisis, 1956*, and by the collapse of his health.

Education Act, 1870 (also known as the 'Forster Act')**:** the creation of the first elementary (primary) state schools, run by locally elected boards.

- The act was the responsibility of W. E. Forster, a minister in *Gladstone*'s 1868–74 government.
- Until 1870, elementary education for the mass of the population was provided mainly by the churches, although these schools had received some money from the state since 1833.
- The church-run 'voluntary system' remained the main vehicle of education, but 'board schools', run by locally elected authorities, were to be created where there were no existing schools. These authorities were known as school boards.
- Board schools were to teach a commonly accepted Christianity, without bias towards any one religious group (non-denominational teaching).
- Elementary education did not become compulsory until 1880 and was not made free until 1891.

Education Act, 1902 (also known as the '*Balfour* Act')**:** the creation of Local Education Authorities (LEAs), run by county councils, with responsibility for elementary and secondary education.

- It was a response to the fact that Britain was behind its main competitors, the USA and Germany, in secondary education.

- The act created Local Education Authorities to replace the old school boards.
- It angered *nonconformists* by providing local financial support (from the rates) for church schools.

Education Act, 1918 (also known as the 'Fisher Act'): an act that raised the school-leaving age from 12 to 14 and planned for the expansion of education beyond that age.

- The act was the responsibility of Herbert Fisher, President of the Board of Education in the *Lloyd George* government.
- It made provision for part-time education for pupils aged 14 to 18. This development was held back by spending cuts (the so-called 'Geddes axe') in 1922.

Education Act, 1944 (also known as the '*Butler* Act'): the creation of a system of secondary education for all children, based on ability assessed at the age of 11 (the '11-plus' test).

- The act ensured that children were sent either to a grammar school (if considered academically inclined) or to a secondary modern or a technical school (if considered to have more practical aptitude). Not all areas had technical schools.
- The school-leaving age was to be raised to 15.
- The 11-plus test was increasingly criticised for unfairly 'pigeon-holing' children at a particular age. In 1965, the Labour government directed local authorities to build comprehensive schools, in which pupils of all abilities would be taught on one site.

Education Act, 1988 (also known as the 'Baker Act'): a series of measures that aimed to establish national standards of teaching and testing of children, and to widen parents' choice of schools.

- The act reflected the ideas of *Thatcherism*, on improving the quality of public service through introducing competition and giving consumers (in this case parents) more power.
- It was the responsibility of Education Secretary Kenneth Baker.
- It created a National Curriculum, with specified content of subjects for all children under the age of 16, and regular testing of pupils at four key stages.
- It allowed schools to opt out of Local Education Authority control. They would become 'grant-maintained schools', receiving money directly from central government and the right to control their own budgets.

EEC: see *European Economic Community.*

Employers and Workmen Act, 1875: see *Conspiracy and Protection of Property Act, 1875.*

Entente Cordiale: see *Anglo–French Agreement, 1904.*

ERM: see *Exchange Rate Mechanism.*

European Economic Community (EEC or Common Market): an alliance of west European states, now enlarged and known as the European Union, of which Britain became a member in 1972.

- The alliance was created by the 1957 Treaty of Rome. The original members were France, Belgium, the Netherlands, West Germany, Italy and Luxembourg. Britain did not originally want to join.

- *Macmillan*'s government reached the conclusion by 1961 that membership would bolster Britain's weakening economy and give it a new international role as the *British empire* was gradually dismantled.
- Two British applications for membership were rejected, in 1963 and 1967, by French President de Gaulle, before the *Heath* government successfully negotiated entry in 1972.
- The purpose of the EEC was to promote economic and political co-operation between member states. In Britain, the growth of European political unity (reflected in the change of name to the European Community and later European Union) has been a cause of controversy. Some politicians have feared a loss of sovereignty (independence) to the Community.
- **TIP** Make sure you know the reasons why Britain was slow to become interested in the Community, and why it eventually decided to apply for membership.

European Union (EU): see *European Economic Community*.

evangelicalism: a religious movement in the Church of England in the 1830s and 1840s, associated with several campaigns for social and moral improvement.

- Evangelicals believed that God was calling them to devote their time to good causes. They held that better social conditions would lift the dignity of the poor and make them more responsive to religion.
- One prominent evangelical was Lord Ashley, later the Earl of Shaftesbury (1801–85), active in campaigns for working-class education and shorter working days in factories (the '10-hour day' campaign).
- Evangelicals had some influence on the reforms passed by the *Whig* governments of the 1830s.

Exchange Rate Mechanism (ERM): a system whereby a number of European countries agreed, after 1979, to establish fixed exchange rates for their currencies.

- A fixed exchange rate is a set rate (or price) at which one currency is exchanged for another. Many people in the business world wanted this because it would give them more stability in international trading.
- British membership of the ERM was popular with pro-Europeans, who saw it as a forerunner of a single currency (the Euro). Some members of the *Thatcher* government, such as Sir Geoffrey Howe (Foreign Secretary 1983–89) and Nigel Lawson (Chancellor of the Exchequer 1983–89), argued that Britain would lack influence in Europe if it did not join.
- Britain joined the ERM in October 1990 but was forced by pressure in the money markets (where currencies are bought and sold) to leave in September 1992 ('Black Wednesday'). This enabled the value of the pound to fall and the British economy recovered. But it damaged the *Major* government's reputation for economic competence and, in the long run, contributed to the Conservative election defeat of 1997.

Fabian Society: a political society, founded in 1884, whose members argued in favour of a gradual transition to socialism, or state ownership of the economy.
- The society mostly consisted of middle-class intellectuals, such as the playwright George Bernard Shaw, who saw private enterprise as wasteful and inefficient. They believed in the superior merits of a socialist society.
- The society did not at first see the need for a separate *Labour Party*, but looked to existing parties to adopt their ideas.
- The Fabian Sidney Webb helped to write Labour's 1918 constitution, which included the famous *Clause Four* commitment to socialism.

Factory Acts: a series of laws regulating the hours and conditions of workers, especially women and children, in mills and factories during the nineteenth century.
- In the nineteenth century, the accepted view was that governments should interfere as little as possible in the relations between employers and employees. However, exceptions were made for female and child workers, whose bargaining power was weaker than that of men.
- The first important Factory Act was passed in 1833. It banned children under the age of 9 from working in textile mills and laid down a 48-hour week for the 9–13 age-group. Inspectors were appointed to enforce the law.
- The 1844 act further reduced children's hours and introduced basic safety requirements.
- In 1847, following a campaign by the *Ten Hours Movement,* a 10-hour day was introduced for women and children.
- These acts applied only to textile factories. Their provisions were extended to other industries in 1867.

fair trade: see *protectionism*.

Falklands War, 1982: a conflict caused by Argentina's attempt to seize control of the Falkland Islands from Britain.
- The Falkland Islands, in the south Atlantic, had been a British colony since 1833 but had been claimed by Argentina. The inhabitants wanted to remain British.
- In April 1982, the Argentinians invaded the islands but were defeated 2 months later by a task force from Britain.

- The victory was presented by Mrs *Thatcher* as a revival of Britain's standing in the world. Some have argued that it helped the Conservatives to win the 1983 general election.

Faulkner, Brian (1921–77): *Ulster Unionist Party* leader and Prime Minister of Northern Ireland 1971–72; Chief Executive of the Power-Sharing Administration, 1974.

- As Northern Ireland Prime Minister during the early stages of the '*Troubles*', Faulkner introduced internment — the practice of arresting suspected *IRA* members and holding them without trial. This policy added to the unpopularity of the Stormont government with the Catholic/Nationalist community. It contributed to the *Heath* government's decision to introduce *direct rule* in March 1972.
- Faulkner supported the *Sunningdale Agreement, 1973*, and headed the short-lived power-sharing administration that it created. His brand of moderate Unionism failed to bridge the gulf between hard-line Unionists and republicans in Northern Ireland.

Fawcett, Millicent (1847–1929): a campaigner for votes for women, who founded the National Union of Women's Suffrage Societies (NUWSS) in 1897.

- Millicent Fawcett was the widow of Henry Fawcett, a *Radical* MP and member of *Gladstone*'s second *Cabinet*. She worked consistently for female suffrage from the 1860s.
- The National Union of Women's Suffrage Societies brought together a number of existing women's pressure groups. It favoured peaceful methods of drawing attention to its demands.
- From 1903, the more militant *Women's Social and Political Union (WSPU)* won greater publicity. Nonetheless, historians consider that the NUWSS played an important part in persuading people of the women's suffrage case. By 1913 it had 50,000 members. Many women preferred its non-violent methods. It put pressure on the *Asquith* government by winning trade union and *Labour Party* support.
- She also founded Newnham, a women's college at Cambridge University, in 1871.

Fenian: a member of an Irish republican movement, founded in the USA in 1858, committed to achieving independence from Britain by violent means.

- Fenians carried out a series of terrorist attacks in Ireland and England in 1867, including incidents at Chester, Manchester and Clerkenwell Jail in London.
- These events helped to draw *Gladstone*'s attention to the problems of Ireland. He determined to carry out a series of reforms designed to win the majority of Irish people away from support for the Fenians.

▪ *TIP* Fenian activity is important background for the study of Gladstone and Ireland between 1868 and 1893.

Festival of Britain, 1951: an exhibition held on London's South Bank to demonstrate Britain's recovery from the Second World War and to show the world its technological and artistic skills.

- The festival marked the centenary of the 1851 Great Exhibition, held in the *Crystal Palace*. It featured a number of modernist buildings and temporary structures, such as the famous Skylon. The Royal Festival Hall, a major arts centre near Waterloo Bridge, survives.
- It was ridiculed by the press and the Conservative opposition as a waste of public money, but it attracted many visitors.
- The Labour government minister in charge was Herbert *Morrison* (1888–1965), grandfather of Peter Mandelson, who was associated with the Millennium Dome at Greenwich.

Foot, Michael (1913–): Employment Secretary 1974–76; Lord President of the Council 1976–79; leader of the *Labour Party* 1980–83.

- Foot was deputy to *Callaghan* in the 1976–79 Labour government. He played an important role in the government's survival in the *House of Commons* as its majority slipped away through a series of by-elections.
- He was elected leader of the party in 1980, after Callaghan's retirement. He won the support of the left wing but was also seen by many moderates as more likely than *Healey* to unite the party. In fact, in 1981 a group of right-wing MPs left to form the *Social Democratic Party*.
- He proved ineffective as leader and led the party to its heaviest defeat since 1935 in the 1983 general election. He allowed the party to fight on a left-wing manifesto, described as 'the longest suicide note in history' by MP Gerald Kaufman. It included proposals for the abandonment of nuclear weapons and a massive extension of state control over the economy.

▓ *TIP* Foot's leadership of the Labour Party helps to explain *Thatcher*'s domination of the politics of the period.

Fox, Charles James (1749–1806): a leading *Whig* politician; Foreign Secretary 1782, 1783, 1806.

- Fox was the leading opponent of *Pitt*, whose political dominance in the 1780s and 1790s he was unable to break.
- He was sympathetic to the ideals behind the *French Revolution* and opposed to Pitt's repression of Radicalism during the French Revolutionary Wars. This position did Fox little good with the property-owning classes and helps to explain why he was so rarely in government. In 1794, right-wing Whigs under the Duke of Portland joined forces with Pitt on the issue of resistance to revolution. Fox led those Whigs who did not join this alliance.

franchise: see *parliamentary reform*.

Franchise Act, 1832 (also known as the 'Great Reform Act'): a reform of the electoral system that made it more broadly representative of industrial society.

- The pre-1832 electoral system allowed fewer than 500,000 men (no women) out of a total population of 24 million the right to vote. In the boroughs (towns) there was a bewildering variety of qualifications for voting.
- This earlier system had not taken account of population movements towards

the new towns of the *Industrial Revolution*. Small boroughs returned two MPs to Parliament, while important centres lacked separate representation.

- The *Whigs* set out to modify this system in order to satisfy middle-class pressure for change and to avoid a revolution.
- The 1832 act, passed by Lord *Grey*'s government, created a uniform property qualification of £10 for voting in the boroughs. This gave the vote to urban business and professional men. The total size of the electorate was now 813,000.
- Small boroughs lost MPs and places such as Manchester and Birmingham gained representation in Parliament.
- Working-class people were still excluded from the vote and the absence of a *secret ballot* meant that landlords continued to have power over elections.
- **TIP** Know the ways in which the act of 1832 modernised the political system, and the ways in which it ensured that the power of the aristocracy was protected.

Franchise Act, 1867: a reform that granted the vote to all male heads of households in boroughs (household suffrage).

- By the late 1860s, there was growing pressure to extend the vote to sections of the working class.
- The Liberals, under *Russell* and *Gladstone*, introduced a bill in 1866 but this was defeated by a combination of Conservatives and Liberal rebels, known as the *Adullamites*.
- The Conservatives, led by *Disraeli* in the *House of Commons*, then surprised their opponents by bringing in their own bill. In its final form it established the principle of household suffrage (the vote for householders) in the boroughs.
- It was condemned by some Conservatives, such as the future Lord *Salisbury*, as a surrender to democracy. It stimulated the growth of formal *Liberal* and *Conservative Party* organisations, designed to win the support of an enlarged electorate.

Franchise Act, 1884: a reform that granted the vote to all male heads of households in the counties — agricultural labourers, miners and others.

- It was passed by *Gladstone*'s second government, in response to pressure for the equalisation of voting qualifications in the boroughs and the counties.
- Approximately 60% of the adult male population was now enfranchised (allowed to vote).
- The Conservatives blocked the bill in the *House of Lords* until the government passed a bill to redistribute constituencies. This meant that MPs now represented areas containing more or less equal numbers of people. Constituencies were generally reduced in size, with one MP each rather than two or more, and they covered areas with distinctly working-class or middle-class voters.
- **TIP** Remember that many working-class men, and all women, were still excluded from voting until 1918. This is relevant to the topic of *Conservative Party* dominance between 1885 and 1905.

Franchise Act, 1918: a reform that gave the vote to all men over the age of 21 and women over the age of 30.

- The act is generally regarded as the arrival of true democracy, although women aged 21 to 30 had to wait until 1928 for equal voting rights with men.
- It increased the number of voters from 8 million to 22 million.
- It recognised women's contribution to the war effort but its main purpose was to give the vote to men who had served in the First World War.
- The voting age was reduced to 18 in 1969.

free fooder: a member of the *Conservative Party*, or of the *Liberal Unionist* Party, who rejected Joseph *Chamberlain*'s proposals for tariffs (taxes) on imported food after 1903.

- Free fooders saw tariffs as a vote-loser in a country attached to the benefits of *free trade*, especially cheap food, since the mid-Victorian period. Many free fooders distrusted Chamberlain, fearing that he wanted to take over the Conservative Party.
- The issue split the party between free fooders, wholehoggers (in favour of tariffs) and moderate supporters of *Balfour*, the Prime Minister.
- Free fooders found themselves pushed to the margins of the Conservative Party. Some, like *Winston Churchill*, became Liberals.

free trade: the idea that goods should be exchanged between countries without a tariff (tax or duty) being paid.

- Free trade was supported by the majority of the business community in the nineteenth century, since it enabled Britain to gain cheap food and raw materials, and to export manufactured goods to a world market in return.
- Some steps towards free trade were taken by *Liverpool*'s government in the 1820s. This was continued by *Peel*'s 1841–46 government and completed by *Gladstone* as Chancellor of the Exchequer.
- Free trade was questioned by some sections of the business world in the late nineteenth century, as Britain's main rivals, the USA and Germany, prospered behind tariff walls.
- The electorate associated free trade with rising living standards and cheap food, and this is why Conservative proposals for tariffs resulted in electoral defeat in 1906 and 1923. The abandonment of free trade did not become acceptable in Britain until the *Great Depression* of the early 1930s.

French Revolution: a period of upheaval in French history, starting in 1789 and leading to the replacement of the monarchy by a republic in 1792.

- French revolutionaries subscribed to the slogan 'liberty, equality, fraternity'. This inspired *Radicals* in Britain, who saw France as a model for change elsewhere. They wanted to end aristocratic domination of society and government.
- Conservatives feared that the violence of the French Revolution could be repeated in Britain. They saw it as a threat to good order and, in the early nineteenth century, it hardened their determination to prevent parliamentary reform and other changes.

- Between 1793 and 1802, Britain took part in the French Revolutionary Wars, in order to resist the spread of revolutionary ideas and to protect British security after French forces moved into the Netherlands.

■ *TIP* The memory of the French Revolution is important for an understanding of the law and order policies of *Liverpool*'s government in the period 1815–20.

Gaitskell, Hugh (1906–63): Chancellor of the Exchequer 1950–51; leader of the *Labour Party* 1955–63.

- As Chancellor in the postwar Labour government, Gaitskell imposed health service charges in his 1951 budget, in order to fund rearmament for the Korean War. This provoked the resignation of *Bevan* and led to a damaging left–right conflict in the Labour Party.
- He was elected Labour leader in 1955, and tried to lead his party away from left-wing policies which were unacceptable to the electorate. He clashed with supporters of unilateral (one-sided) nuclear disarmament at the 1960 Scarborough party conference. In 1961 he tried to end Labour's historic commitment to *Clause Four* socialism.
- Gaitskell has sometimes been claimed as a forerunner of the 1990s modernisers associated with *Blair*.
- He died suddenly in January 1963 and was succeeded as leader by *Wilson*.

Gandhi, Mohandas (Mahatma) (1869–1948): an Indian nationalist leader who led the Indian National Congress movement, whose aim was independence from British rule.

- Gandhi practised as a lawyer in South Africa, where he championed the rights of the Asian community, before returning to India.
- He led the Indian National Congress movement from 1921 and organised a strategy of passive, non-violent resistance to British rule, in pursuit of Indian independence.
- He opposed the partition of India into two states, India and Pakistan, in 1947.
- Gandhi was assassinated by a Hindu fanatic within a year of independence.

General Strike, 1926: a period of 9 days when the great majority of trade union members went on strike in support of the coal miners, who were in dispute with their employers.

- The background to the strike was the determination of the coal-mine owners to impose wage cuts, in response to declining coal exports. The *Baldwin* government appointed a royal commission to investigate the problems of the coal industry and maintained the men's wages from 1925 to 1926.
- Mine owners and miners failed to reach agreement, and negotiations between

government and *Trades Union Congress (TUC)* representatives broke down in May 1926. Other workers stopped work in support of the miners but they were not equipped for a long strike. The government was well prepared and used its control of the radio to denounce the General Strike as a threat to lawful authority.

- After the collapse of the General Strike, the miners stayed out for another 7 months before accepting the owners' terms. This was a massive defeat for industrial action as a weapon against employers and government.

Gladstone, William Ewart (1809–98): Chancellor of the Exchequer 1852–55, 1859–66; Prime Minister 1868–74, 1880–85, 1886, 1892–94; leader of the *Liberal Party* 1868–94.

- Gladstone began his career as a Conservative and followed *Peel* when the party split over repeal of the *Corn Laws* in 1846.
- He moved to the Liberals in the 1850s, after finding common ground with them on a variety of issues. As Chancellor, he reduced or abolished duties on many imported goods and kept a tight rein on public expenditure.
- His first government carried out a number of important reforms, opening up the Army and civil service to promotion by merit and introducing the *Education Act, 1870.*
- As Liberal leader, Gladstone was an inspiring speaker of deep religious conviction, who united his party behind uplifting moral issues, such as his campaign against *Disraeli*'s *imperialism* in 1879–80. Opponents accused him of an unpatriotic 'little England' outlook.
- His conversion to *Home Rule* for Ireland in 1885–86 split the Liberal Party and kept it out of power for most of the next two decades.

■ *TIP* Gladstone's religious beliefs are a key to understanding his outlook and his differences with his more worldly and cynical rival, Disraeli.

Gladstonian Liberalism: the outlook of the *Liberal Party* under the leadership of *Gladstone*, between the 1860s and the 1890s.

- This form of liberalism sought a limited role for government in the economy and society. Public expenditure and taxation were to be kept low in order to reward individual effort and help business. Artificial restrictions on trade, such as protective tariffs, were to be abolished.
- The efficiency of government and other public institutions, such as the civil service and judicial system, was to be improved.
- International peace was to be promoted by maintaining limited armed forces and keeping out of foreign disputes.
- It was not the job of government to help one class or group at the expense of others. Given the varied composition of the nineteenth-century Liberal Party, Gladstone sought to maintain unity by focusing his supporters' energies on moral crusades, such as justice for the victims of the *Bulgarian atrocities, 1876.*

Goderich, Viscount (Frederick Robinson, later 1st Earl of Ripon) (1782–1859): President of the Board of Trade 1818–23; Chancellor of the Exchequer 1823–27; Prime Minister 1827–28.

- Goderich was a *Liberal Tory* who took important steps towards a policy of *free trade* as a member of *Liverpool*'s government. He became known as 'Prosperity Robinson'.
- He became Prime Minister on the death of *Canning*, but failed to provide stable government and resigned without meeting Parliament. This contributed to the disintegration of the *Tory Party* in 1828–30.
- He later served in *Grey*'s *Whig* government before returning to the Conservatives to serve under *Peel* in his 1841–46 government.

gold standard: a monetary system under which a national currency had a fixed value in gold.

- Britain belonged to the gold standard until the First World War, when problems of wartime finance forced it to allow the pound to have a flexible value.
- Britain returned to the gold standard in 1925, in the belief that a fixed value was essential to restore the confidence of investors. The rate of exchange (£1 = $4.86) was too high for postwar conditions and made it hard for British exporters to sell their goods abroad.
- The second Labour government faced a collapse of confidence in the pound in August 1931. Its members believed that they must keep to the gold standard but could not agree on a package of economy cuts, necessary if Britain was to be given a loan by foreign bankers. The government resigned and was replaced by a *National Government*.
- The National Government was forced to abandon the gold standard when its announcement of spending cuts triggered a mutiny at the Invergordon naval base in September and caused a financial panic.
- The value of the pound stabilised at $3.40 and allowed a reduction of interest rates, thereby contributing to recovery from the *Great Depression*.

▦ *TIP* An understanding of the gold standard is important for the problems of Britain's interwar economy.

Good Friday Agreement, 1998: an attempt to end the conflict in Northern Ireland through the creation of an assembly representing all parties.

- The agreement was the outcome of a 'peace process' that began when the Provisional *IRA* agreed to a cease-fire following the election of the Labour government in 1997.
- Most of the Northern Ireland parties, including *Sinn Fein*, agreed to the terms. These included acceptance of the principle that Northern Ireland's place in the UK depends on the consent of its people.
- The agreement created an assembly for Northern Ireland and an executive (government) containing *Unionist* and Sinn Fein ministers.
- It remains to be seen whether the agreement has made permanent peace possible. It has been opposed by sections of the Unionist community. The IRA's reluctance to decommission (put out of action) its terrorist weapons has been a cause of argument.

- The negotiation of the agreement was supported by the government of the Irish Republic.

Gordon, General Charles (also known as 'Gordon of Khartoum') **(1833–85):** a British military hero whose murder in the Sudan caused serious embarrassment to *Gladstone*'s second government.

- The Sudan was historically part of Egypt, which Britain took over in 1882. A Muslim nationalist leader, the Mahdi, tried to drive the Egyptian and Western forces out of the Sudan.
- Gladstone's government sent General Gordon to carry out the withdrawal of Anglo–Egyptian troops from the Sudan. Gordon disregarded his orders and remained in the capital, Khartoum, where he was killed by the Mahdi's followers.
- Gladstone's slowness to send a relief expedition to help Gordon made him intensely unpopular. His nickname, the Grand Old Man (GOM), was turned round to read Murderer of Gordon (MOG).

▌ *TIP* The Gordon episode is a useful illustration of the growing public support for *imperialism* in late-Victorian Britain.

Government of India Act, 1919 (also known as the 'Montagu-Chelmsford reforms'): an attempt to keep India within the *British empire*, by making some concessions to nationalists who were seeking independence for their country.

- The act followed an announcement by India Secretary Edwin Montagu that Britain intended to move gradually towards 'responsible government' for India.
- It gave Indians responsibility for education, public health and agriculture, while leaving the key areas of public order, finance and foreign relations in the hands of the Viceroy, who governed India on behalf of the British Crown.
- It reflected the unwillingness of the British authorities to trust the Indians with full self-government. It was believed that India, with its rival Hindu and Muslim communities, would easily descend into violence.
- The main nationalist movement, the Indian National Congress, responded by organising a campaign of civil disobedience (non-violent protest) against British rule.

Government of India Act, 1935: an attempt to calm Indian nationalist agitation for independence from Britain, by giving more responsibility to Indians at local level.

- The act granted control of the provinces to Indians. Control over foreign affairs, defence, trade and the protection of minorities was reserved for the Viceroy, who governed India as the representative of the British Crown.
- The Hindu-dominated Indian National Congress succeeded in the elections held in eight out of India's eleven provinces. This alarmed the Muslim minority. Congress continued to desire independence for India.
- In Britain, the passage of the act was bitterly opposed by the right wing of the *Conservative Party*, led by *Winston Churchill*. They saw it as likely to lead to the loss of India from the *British empire*.

Government of Ireland Act, 1920: an attempt by the British government to end its conflict with the Irish republican movement by creating two parliaments, one for Northern Ireland, the other for the south.

- Only the Northern Ireland Parliament was created. It was based at Stormont, a suburb of the main city, Belfast.
- In Southern Ireland, *Sinn Fein* rejected the idea of a parliament with limited powers. Irish republicans wanted total independence from Britain. The struggle against Britain continued until the signing of the *Anglo–Irish Treaty, 1921*.

Great Depression: a slump in world trade that affected Britain in the 1920s and the first half of the 1930s.

- Immediately after the First World War, there was a short period when British goods were in demand and the economy boomed. From 1920, demand fell and brought down prices. At the same time, primary producing countries, which depended on exporting food and raw materials, experienced a price fall. These countries were therefore no longer able to afford British manufactured goods. This worsened the position of old established *staple industries*, such as cotton and coal, which were already suffering from problems of lost markets, outdated technology and poor organisation.
- In October 1929, the US Stock Market collapsed (the Wall Street Crash), leading to a further contraction of world trade.
- The main consequence of the Great Depression in Britain was mass un-employment in areas traditionally dependent on heavy industry (northern England, south Wales, Scotland). Southern England and the Midlands, where newer, light industries (such as motor car manufacture and electrical engineering) were located, were affected much less.

Great Exhibition: see *Crystal Palace*.

Great Power: one of the important European countries that dominated inter-national affairs prior to the First World War.

- There were five Great Powers: Great Britain, France, Russia, Austria (known as Austria-Hungary from 1867 to 1918) and Prussia (which developed into Germany in 1871).
- They were the main participants in the *congress system* of the period 1814–25.
- Rivalries between Great Powers led to major conflicts such as the *Crimean War* and the First World War.

Great Reform Act: see *Franchise Act, 1832*.

Grey, Charles, Earl Grey (1764–1845): Foreign Secretary 1806–07; Prime Minister 1830–34.

- Charles Grey was a member of an old Northumberland aristocratic family and a *Whig* in politics. An associate of *Fox*, he spent most of his career in opposition to Tory governments.
- He was a strong believer in reforming the old electoral system, and argued that reform was the only way of avoiding revolution.
- He became Prime Minister at a time of great instability. He carried the *Franchise*

Act, 1832, which aimed to bring the middle classes into the political system.

Grey, Sir Edward (1862–1933): Foreign Secretary 1905–16.

- Edward Grey was a *Liberal imperialist* and a friend and political colleague of *Asquith.*
- As Foreign Secretary, Grey developed close relations with France, although he stopped short of a formal alliance.
- He negotiated an agreement with Russia in 1907, resolving an outstanding dispute over Persia (now Iran).
- His policies encouraged the French to believe that they could rely on British military and naval co-operation in a conflict with Germany. His primary concern was to maintain the *balance of power* in Europe against German aggression.
- In August 1914, he took Britain into war with Germany, following the German invasion of Belgium.

TIP Grey's policies are important for the theme of Anglo–German rivalry prior to 1914. Some of his contemporaries (and later historians) criticised him for involving Britain in war and for the secrecy of his diplomacy.

habeas corpus: an ancient civil liberty, which protected people from being held in prison for long periods without being charged with an offence.

- The term comes from a Latin phrase meaning literally, 'you have the body'.
- This right was suspended by the *Liverpool* government in 1817–18, at a time of intense *Radical* activity. This enabled the authorities to detain those considered guilty of anti-government behaviour for an unspecified period.
- The suspension was widely condemned by Radicals as an attack on civil liberties. Nonetheless, it was a temporary measure and hardly amounted to a thoroughgoing reign of terror.

Hague, William (1961–): Welsh Secretary 1995–97; leader of the *Conservative Party* since 1997.

- Hague succeeded *Major* as Conservative leader following the 1997 general election defeat.
- He launched a campaign to recruit more and younger members to the Conservative Party and changed the rules for party leadership elections, opening voting to all party members, not just MPs.
- He found it hard to establish himself in face of a Labour government with a large majority, and with a Conservative Party still divided over Britain's role in Europe.
- He tried to connect the party with voters under the slogan 'Common Sense Revolution', marking out clear-cut Conservative positions on law and order and opposition to the European single currency (the Euro).
- He has been accused by pro-European Conservatives of turning the party into a narrow right-wing pressure group.

Haldane, Richard Burdon (Viscount Haldane) (1856–1928): War Secretary 1905–12; Lord Chancellor 1912–15, 1924.

- Haldane was a *Liberal imperialist* and an associate of *Sir Edward Grey* and *Asquith.*
- As War Secretary in the Liberal government, he created an Imperial General Staff to direct military campaigns. He also formed the Territorial Army into an effective reserve force and made it possible for Britain to send the *British Expeditionary Force (BEF)* to the continent in 1914.

- He was unfairly attacked by the right-wing press as pro-German, and was dropped from government when Asquith formed a *coalition* with the Conservatives in May 1915.
- He later moved from the *Liberal Party* to Labour and held office in the first Labour government in January–October 1924.

Halifax (Edward Wood, later Lord Irwin), 1st Earl: Viceroy of India 1926–31; War Secretary 1935; Lord Privy Seal 1935–37; Lord President of the Council 1937–38; Foreign Secretary 1938–40.

- As Viceroy of India, Halifax made an important announcement in 1929 — that India's destiny was to gain *Dominion* status. He responded to the growth of Indian nationalism with a readiness to negotiate with its main representative, *Gandhi.*
- After his return to British politics, he was closely associated with *appeasement,* although he had doubts about the policy by 1938 as a way of avoiding war with Germany.
- He was the most popular choice for Prime Minister with Conservatives when *Neville Chamberlain* resigned in May 1940. He stood aside for *Churchill* and ended his career as wartime ambassador to the USA.

Hardie, James Keir (1856–1915): founded the Scottish Labour Party in 1888 and the *Independent Labour Party* in 1893; first chairman of the Parliamentary *Labour Party* 1906–08.

- Hardie was a Scottish miner who began as a Liberal but from the late 1880s worked to create a separate voice in Parliament for working-class people.
- He was one of three independent Labour candidates elected to Parliament in the 1892 general election. He represented West Ham South in the East End of London.
- He was committed to international peace and strongly opposed to Britain's involvement in the First World War.

■ *TIP* A knowledge of Hardie's career and ideas is important for study of the foundation of the Labour Party.

Hartington, Lord (8th Duke of Devonshire from 1891) (1833–1908): Irish Secretary 1871–74; leader of the *Liberal Party* in the Commons 1875–80; India Secretary 1880–82; War Secretary 1882–85; Lord President of the Council 1895–1903.

- Hartington was a leading *Whig* member of *Gladstone*'s first two governments. He refused to serve in 1886 because of his opposition to *Home Rule* for Ireland.
- He became leader of the *Liberal Unionists*, serving under Conservative prime ministers 1895–1903.
- He resigned from *Balfour*'s government in 1903, in opposition to *Joseph Chamberlain*'s proposals for *tariff reform*, and became leader of the *free fooders*.

Healey, Denis (1917–): Defence Secretary 1964–70; Chancellor of the Exchequer 1974–79; deputy leader of the *Labour Party* 1980–83.

- Healey was a key figure in the September 1976 *International Monetary Fund (IMF)* crisis. A collapse of confidence in the pound forced the government to seek a loan from the IMF. The condition of this was that the government had to introduce public-spending cuts, which angered the left wing of the Labour Party.

- He continued to play a role in Labour politics in opposition, as the party moved to the left under the leadership of Michael *Foot* (1980–83). Healey came from Labour's centre-right and seemed unconvincing as deputy leader of a party now committed to unilateral (one-sided) nuclear disarmament and withdrawal from the *EEC*.

Heath, Edward (1916–): Chief Whip 1955–59; Minister of Labour 1959–60; as Lord Privy Seal, in charge of application to join the *EEC*, 1960–63; Secretary for Industry, Trade and Regional Development 1963–64; Prime Minister 1970–74; leader of the *Conservative Party* 1965–75.

- Heath was the first Conservative leader to be elected by a ballot of the party's MPs. He was chosen for his middle-class, grammar-school background and the belief that he would modernise the party's appeal and promote efficiency in government. He was seen as a contrast to old-style aristocratic Conservatives such as *Douglas-Home*.
- He lost the 1966 general election to Labour, but was elected Prime Minister in 1970.
- His major achievement was to lead Britain into the EEC in 1972. He was a consistent supporter of greater European unity.
- His government was hit by problems of inflation and industrial relations. Attempt to control wages and prices led to conflict with the miners' union and to defeat in the February 1974 general election. After further defeat in October 1974, he lost the party leadership to *Thatcher*.

Hedgers and Ditchers: popular names given to the two groups of Conservatives who took up opposing positions on the *Parliament Act, 1911*.

- Hedgers were moderates who were prepared to allow the Parliament Bill to pass, rather than have the *Asquith* government create more Liberal peers in order to force it through. They argued that there would then be a permanent Liberal majority in the *House of Lords*, which would cause further damage to Conservative interests. The most prominent Hedger was Lord Curzon, former Viceroy of India.
- Ditchers (in the sense of 'dying in the last ditch') were those who were prepared to vote against the bill, regardless of the consequences. They were led by Lord Halsbury, an elderly former Lord Chancellor. Their number included *Austen Chamberlain*.
- *Balfour's* failure as party leader to give his backing to the Ditchers damaged him in the eyes of the right wing and contributed to his loss of the leadership in November 1911.

Henderson, Arthur (1863–1935): President of the Board of Education 1915–16; Paymaster-General 1916; member of *Lloyd George*'s War Cabinet 1916–17; Home Secretary 1924; Foreign Secretary 1929–31; leader of the *Labour Party* 1931–32.

- Henderson was the first member of the Labour Party to serve as a government minister, in the 1915–16 *Asquith coalition*.
- After resignation from Lloyd George's War Cabinet, he devoted himself to reorganisation of the Labour Party, encouraging the growth of local branches and making possible an expansion of membership.
- His trade union background gave him a strong sense of loyalty to the party's rank and file. This led him to oppose *MacDonald*'s proposals for cuts in unemployment benefit during the August 1931 financial crisis. He led the group of ministers whose resignations broke up the second Labour government, and he was defeated in the 1931 general election.

Heseltine, Michael (1933–): Environment Secretary 1979–83, 1990–92; Defence Secretary 1983–86; Trade and Industry Secretary 1992–95; deputy Prime Minister 1995–97.

- Heseltine is a flamboyant Conservative politician, a popular and dramatic speaker at party conferences — popularly known as 'Tarzan'.
- Heseltine's pro-European outlook and preference for direct government intervention in social and economic issues led to differences with *Thatcher*.
- He resigned from the government in January 1986 over the Westland affair. The surface issue was his disagreement with the *Cabinet*'s decision to allow the sale of the failing Westland helicopter firm to a US consortium. It also involved his dislike of Thatcher's style of Cabinet management. He felt that his own proposal for a European rescue bid had been unfairly sidelined.
- He challenged Thatcher for the Conservative leadership in November 1990. Although he failed to succeed her, he opened the way for *Major*, in whose government he became a key figure.

Hillsborough Agreement: see *Anglo–Irish Agreement, 1985*.

Hoare–Laval Pact: see *Abyssinian War, 1935–36*.

Home Rule: a proposal to give Ireland its own parliament within the UK.

- Home Rule was the key issue in British politics between the 1880s and the 1920s.
- It was the main demand of the *Irish Nationalist Party*.
- It split the *Liberal Party*, when its leader, *Gladstone*, decided to support the proposal from the end of 1885.
- Three Home Rule bills were introduced into Parliament, in 1886, 1893 and 1912. None became law.
- Conservative and *Liberal Unionist* opponents believed that Home Rule might lead to the break-up of the *British empire*. Some feared that Roman Catholics would dominate the Irish Parliament and that this would lead to discrimination against Protestants.
- ▬ *TIP* Home Rule is an important topic in Gladstone's Irish policy, 1868–93, and in the Liberal governments of 1905–14. Between 1912 and 1914, Home Rule almost led to civil war in Ireland.

Hornby v. Close, 1867: a legal judgement which threatened the security of funds accumulated by a trade union.

- Trade unionists contributed money to a common fund, from which the union could draw in time of need.
- The *House of Lords* ruled that no action could be taken against an official who had absconded with the union's funds.
- This called into question the legal status of trade unions and led to working-class pressure for a change in the law. Trade unions received legal recognition in 1871 from *Gladstone*'s first government.

Hotel Cecil: a nickname applied to the Conservative government of *Salisbury* after about 1900, implying that he promoted his relatives (members of the Cecil family) to an unjustified degree.

- The charge was underlined in 1902 when Salisbury's nephew, *Balfour*, succeeded him as Prime Minister. Salisbury's first name was Robert, hence the saying 'Bob's your uncle'.

House of Commons: the elected part of the British Parliament. By the nineteenth century, it was established as more important than the *House of Lords.*

- The House of Commons has the right of consent to taxation. This explains why the Chancellor of the Exchequer is the one government minister who must always be a member of the Commons.
- Its meetings are chaired by the (neutral) Speaker of the House or by a Deputy Speaker.
- A series of *Franchise Acts* — in 1832, 1867, 1884 and 1918 — reduced and eventually removed the requirement that property ownership was necessary for a person to take part in elections to the Commons.
- In the nineteenth century, governments were often made and unmade by votes in the Commons — for example, the fall of the *Palmerston* government in 1858, or that of *Gladstone* in 1885. This became less common in the twentieth century.
- General elections had to be held every 7 years, until this was reduced to 5 years by the *Parliament Act, 1911.* In addition, an election had to be held on the death of the monarch. The last time that this applied was in 1837.

House of Lords: the upper house of Parliament, which by 1800 was seen as less important than the *House of Commons.*

- The historic House of Lords consisted of hereditary peers, who had inherited their titles, together with Church of England bishops and senior judges. Monarchs, acting on the advice of government ministers, created new hereditary peers with the right to sit in the House of Lords. The first life peers were appointed in 1958.
- The House of Lords is chaired by the Lord Chancellor, the country's most senior judge, who is also a *Cabinet* minister.
- Most of the hereditary peers were removed from the Lords in 1999 by the *Blair* government, which was committed to the modernisation of the British political system.

- Until the passage of the *Parliament Act, 1911,* the Lords possessed the right to veto (vote down) laws started by the House of Commons. After that date, they were allowed to delay bills for 2 years and were banned from hindering money bills at all. The delaying power was reduced to 1 year in 1949.

humanitarian: a member of a cross-party movement in the 1830s and 1840s that sought to improve the conditions of industrial workers and others.

- Humanitarians had a strong social conscience and were appalled by the long hours and poor working conditions of many factory workers.
- The movement included compassionate Tories such as Lord Ashley (later Earl of Shaftesbury) as well as followers of *Chartism.*
- It influenced the passing of laws such as the 1833 *Factory Act.*

Hunt, Henry ('Orator') (1773–1835): a *Radical* politician who campaigned for universal male suffrage (votes for all men) and was arrested at *Peterloo* in 1819.

- A well-known opponent of *Liverpool*'s Tory government, Hunt was the main speaker at the Peterloo meeting at Manchester in 1819. He was arrested and jailed for 2 years for his part in the episode.
- He was known as 'Orator' Hunt because of his ability to rouse crowds through public speaking.
- As an MP from 1830 to 1833, he opposed the *Franchise Act, 1832* for its failure to give the vote to working-class men.

Huskisson, William (1770–1830): President of the Board of Trade 1823–27; Colonial Secretary and leader of the *House of Commons* 1828.

- Huskisson was a *Liberal Tory* who carried several measures of *free trade* as a member of *Liverpool*'s government.
- He became leader of the followers of *Canning* after the latter's death in August 1827.
- He resigned from *Wellington*'s government following a disagreement over the allocation of two parliamentary seats to new industrial areas. This weakened the unity of the *Tory Party.*
- He was killed at the opening of the Liverpool to Manchester railway, becoming the first rail accident victim.

IMF: see *International Monetary Fund*.

Imperialism: the practice of extending a country's power and influence over other territories; the urge to build an empire.

● For much of the nineteenth century, British influence was promoted largely through 'informal empire' — through trade and other means short of the physical conquest of territory. This began to change from about 1880, as Britain established formal control of many areas, especially in Africa.

● Some historians have interpreted the growth of empire purely in economic terms, as part of an urge to find new markets and cheap raw materials, or as an outlet for investment overseas. This interpretation was challenged in the 1960s by two historians, Ronald Robinson and Jack Gallagher, who argued that imperial expansion was driven by a need to safeguard the route to India, which was threatened by localised disturbances in Egypt in 1882.

● *TIP* Familiarise yourself with the main arguments behind Britain's acquisition of new territory in the late nineteenth century. Remember that not all historians accept the Robinson/Gallagher thesis.

imperial preference: see *tariff reform*.

incomes policy: one of a series of attempts by post-1945 Conservative and Labour governments to restrain wage demands in order to hold down *inflation*.

● Governments tried to reach agreement with the trade unions on what was an acceptable level of wage increase, in the wider interests of the economy.

● Both the *Heath* and *Callaghan* governments were brought down by union rejection of their incomes policies.

● The *Thatcher* government decided to leave the market to determine wage levels.

income tax: a tax on how much a person earns, originally introduced as a temporary measure to finance the war against revolutionary France in 1797.

● Income tax is an example of direct taxation, as opposed to indirect taxation (duties on goods). The latter bears no relation to a person's wealth.

● Income tax was abolished after the end of the French Wars in 1816. This was the result of pressure from wealthy landowning MPs, on whom it had mainly fallen.

● It was reintroduced by *Peel* in 1842 at the rate of 7 pence in the pound, on annual incomes over £150. This yielded a budget surplus for the government and enabled it to abolish duties on many items. (Note: before the introduction of the decimal system of currency in 1971, there were 240 pence in the pound.)

- Income tax became a permanent fixture, although before the First World War only members of the upper and middle classes had to pay it.

Independent Labour Party: an alliance of various socialist groups, formed in January 1893, to promote the interests of working-class people.

- The ILP was founded by *Hardie* at a conference in Bradford, West Yorkshire. It was attended by socialist societies, including the *Fabians* and the *Social Democratic Federation*.
- Members believed in the socialist principle of common (state) ownership of the economy, but they also campaigned for more limited objectives, such as an 8-hour working day.
- Support for the party was strongest in the industrial north of England. It did not, however, win the support of the mass of the trade union movement.
- It provided the starting-point for the careers of *MacDonald, Snowden* and others. It also helped to create the Labour Representation Committee (later the *Labour Party*) in 1900.

■ *TIP* For exam questions on the origins of the Labour Party, you will need to know what the ILP stood for and what its strengths and weaknesses were.

Indian independence, 1947: the decision by the *Attlee* government to end British rule of India.

- The main pressure for British withdrawal from India came from the Indian National Congress. This body, which mainly represented the majority Hindu community, was formed in 1885 but did not become a major force until after the First World War, under the leadership of *Gandhi*.
- Britain was committed to eventual *Dominion* status for India from 1929, but this did not satisfy Congress. During the Second World War and immediately after, Britain found it hard to control mounting opposition to its rule.
- The situation was complicated by the fears of the Muslims, who were concentrated mainly in the north, that they would suffer in a Hindu-dominated independent India. The Muslim League, led by Muhammad Ali Jinnah, campaigned for a separate state in the north.
- The Attlee government decided to grant independence, and sent *Mountbatten* out as the last Viceroy to organise the transfer of power. He concluded that there was no alternative to partition between Hindus and Muslims. Two states, India and Pakistan, came into being in August 1947 amid violent conflict between the two communities.

Indian mutiny, 1857: a rebellion against British rule, by sections of the Indian Army.

- Britain had made use of native troops (sepoys), employed by the East India Company, in controlling India. Insensitive decisions, which offended the religious beliefs of both Hindu and Muslim troops, triggered a revolt against the imperial power. More generally, there was resentment against the spread of Western influence.

- British opinion was appalled by stories of atrocities carried out by the rebels, such as the massacre of European women and children at Cawnpore. The mutiny was suppressed with great ferocity.
- The mutiny called into question the wisdom of relying on a trading company as an agent of British rule. In 1858, the administration of British India was transferred to a *Cabinet* minister, the India Secretary, and to the Viceroy, who represented the Crown in India. This system was essentially the one under which India was governed until it became independent in 1947.

Industrial Relations Act, 1971: an attempt by *Heath*'s Conservative government to prevent strikes and bring the trade union movement under legal restraint.

- The act required unions to hold a ballot of their members before calling a strike. A National Industrial Relations Court was set up to enforce the act.
- The act was bitterly opposed by the trade unions, who had not been consulted about its provisions. It was widely defied, and was repealed by the next Labour government.

Industrial Revolution: the process of economic change that took place in Britain between about 1750 and 1850, and which led to the majority of the working population moving from agriculture to manufacturing industry.

- It involved a change from mainly domestic (cottage) industry, catering for a small market, to industry based in large factory units and supplying a mass market.
- It was accompanied by the growth of large urban settlements, such as Manchester and Birmingham, which had previously lacked importance.
- The new routines of factory work and the growth of closely packed industrial slum housing led to widening social divisions between middle and working classes.
- The transfer of population from countryside to towns made it necessary for agriculture to improve its productivity and to adopt new, more efficient methods.

inflation: a sustained increase in the level of prices, leading to a reduction of the purchasing power of money.

- Inflation can be caused by a shortage of raw materials or of goods, which leads to increased demand and therefore pushes prices up. Alternatively, it may occur when wage increases are not matched by increases in productivity — i.e. when people are paid more than they really earn.
- Those who live on pensions and fixed incomes are hit harder by inflation than are wage earners.
- The disastrous German inflation of 1923, when the value of money collapsed, caused fears of a similar crisis in Britain. This was a factor in the election of the *National Government* in October 1931.

- Inflation became a serious problem in Britain in the 1970s. An important feature of *Thatcherism* was the commitment to dealing with inflation by controlling the amount of money in circulation in the economy. This was achieved at a cost of job losses and the collapse of large sections of manufacturing industry.

'In Place of Strife', 1969: proposals by the *Wilson* government to impose controls on trade unions and their right to strike.

- The proposals were the work of Employment Secretary Barbara Castle, supported by Wilson as Prime Minister. It was surprising for a Labour government to seek to discipline the trade unions.
- The proposals caused controversy within the Labour movement and inside the *Cabinet*, where opposition was led by *Callaghan*, the Home Secretary. They were dropped.
- The government signed a 'solemn and binding undertaking' with the *Trades Union Congress (TUC)*, which promised to use its influence in the interests of industrial peace. This failed to stop the industrial disputes of the 1970s and paved the way for the more drastic trade union law reforms of the *Thatcher* government.

International Monetary Fund (IMF): an organisation created to help world trade and promote exchange rate stability after the Second World War.

- The IMF operated a gold and currency reserve system, available to member countries to help them overcome *balance of payments* problems.
- The *Callaghan* government had to apply for an IMF loan in 1976, after a lack of confidence in the pound led to a serious fall in its value in the international money markets. The government negotiated a $3.9 billion loan in return for a £4.5 billion cut in public expenditure.
- This crisis damaged Britain's image in the eyes of the world. It caused controversy within the *Labour Party*, whose left wing regarded the spending cuts as a betrayal of their working-class supporters.

IRA: see *Irish Republican Army*.

Irish famine, 1845–49: a scarcity of food, caused by repeated failure of the potato crop, with catastrophic results for the Irish population.

- The Irish peasant farming population was dependent on the potato, which was hit by a blight in successive years. Approximately 1 million people died and another million emigrated, mainly to the USA.
- Great anger was caused in Ireland by the inadequacy of the famine relief arrangements and the apparent indifference of the British government towards Irish suffering.
- The outbreak of the famine influenced the timing of *Peel*'s decision to repeal the *Corn Laws* in 1846.
- *TIP* The Irish famine is important to an understanding of the growth of Irish nationalism, because of its emotional importance to those who settled in the USA and supported movements for the independence of their country of origin.

Irish Land Acts, 1870 and 1881: laws passed by *Gladstone*'s governments in an effort to improve the conditions of the Irish tenant farming community.

● The 1870 Act extended to other parts of Ireland a custom existing in Ulster (northern Ireland) whereby tenants were able to claim compensation from their landlord for improvements made to their land holding. It failed to curb evictions of tenants who could not pay their rent in times of hardship.

● The 1881 Act went further in interfering with the property rights of Irish landlords. It established the 'three Fs': fair rent, to be fixed by a court, in the event of a dispute between landlord and tenant; free sale of a tenant's interest in his holding when he moved to a new farm; and fixity of tenure.

■ *TIP* Be sure not to confuse the details of these two important acts.

Irish Land Purchase Acts: laws passed by Conservative governments in 1885, 1887, 1891 and 1903, providing state assistance to tenant farmers who wished to buy their land holdings.

● These acts tried to bring stability to rural Ireland by creating a new class of small landowners. The idea was that the peasant farmers would be less likely to oppose British rule if they had a stake in the land.

● The 1885 (Ashbourne) Act allowed tenants an advance of the sum needed to buy land, which was to be repaid over 49 years at 4% interest. The 1887 and 1891 acts increased the amount of money available for this purpose.

● The most far-reaching act was passed in 1903 and was the work of Irish Secretary George Wyndham. By 1909, 300,000 tenant farmers (out of a total of 500,000) were in the process of buying their own farms.

Irish Nationalist Party (also known as the 'Home Rule Party')**:** a political party founded in 1870 to campaign for a parliament for Ireland.

● The party was founded by *Butt* in 1870 as the Home Government Association. From the late 1870s, it developed a more militant approach under the leadership of *Parnell*, obstructing the passage of non-Irish bills in the *House of Commons* in order to draw attention to its demands.

● It reached a high point of influence in British politics when the *Liberal Party* under *Gladstone* became committed to *Home Rule* in 1885–86. It kept Liberal governments in power from 1892 to 1895 and 1910 to 1915.

● The INP declined in influence between 1916 and 1918, being replaced as the main voice of Irish nationalism by the republican *Sinn Fein*.

Irish Question: a convenient term for the complex of religious, political and social issues which created a difficult relationship between Britain and Ireland in the nineteenth century.

● Although 80% of the Irish population was Catholic, the greater part of the wealth and power was concentrated in the hands of the Protestant minority. Protestants were numerically strongest in the north of Ireland (Ulster) and were determined to maintain their position within the UK.

● The south and west were mainly rural, and conditions were poor for the majority of the inhabitants. Irish tenant farmers experienced low status and limited security as a result of the domination of an Anglo–Irish landlord class. By contrast, the north was industrialising rapidly and enjoyed a quality of life similar to that of mainland Britain.

- Irish nationalists, who were strongest in the south, campaigned for *Home Rule*. The British government was resistant to this because it feared that British security and the safety of the empire might be threatened.

TIP Exam questions on the failure of British politicians to solve the Irish Question between 1800 and 1921 will require an opening explanation of the main features of the problem.

Irish Republican Army (IRA): a terrorist organisation, adopting the terminology of a regular army, whose aim has been the forcible incorporation of Northern Ireland into a united Ireland.

- The IRA was formed in 1919. It developed out of an earlier organisation, the Irish Volunteers. It purpose was to fight for independence against the forces of the British government.

- The Catholic movement for civil rights in Northern Ireland, which became important in 1968–69, created a new opportunity for the IRA. A group of militants, led by Sean MacStiofain, formed the Provisional IRA to engage in armed defence of the Catholic community against the Protestant-dominated Stormont government.

- The Provisional IRA aimed to bring about British withdrawal from Northern Ireland by means of terrorist attacks, both there and on the British mainland. These continued until the cease-fire of 1994 (broken in 1996 and renewed in 1997), a tactical manoeuvre prompted by signs of an increased willingness on the part of the British government to find a political solution.

Irish Universities Bill, 1873: a proposal by *Gladstone*'s Liberal government to create a new centre of higher education in Ireland, in order to satisfy the Catholic population.

- The bill was not drafted in consultation with the leaders of the Catholic Church in Ireland, who wanted a purely Catholic university.

- In an attempt to avoid conflict between Protestants and Catholics, the bill excluded certain subjects (theology, philosophy, modern history) from the curriculum. This antagonised Liberals, who believed in open discussion.

- The bill did not become law. Its defeat was a serious setback for the Gladstone government.

TIP The failure of the bill is an important episode in the history of nineteenth-century Ireland, and in the career of Gladstone.

Jameson raid, 1895: a failed attempt by Dr Leander Starr Jameson, agent for Cecil *Rhodes*'s British South Africa Company, to start a rising of British settlers against the Boer (of Dutch origin) government of the Transvaal Republic.

- Mineral prospectors in the Transvaal, mainly of British background ('Uitlanders'), were taxed by the Boer government, although denied voting rights. Cecil Rhodes, a millionaire entrepreneur, was anxious to extend his influence in southern Africa and was supported by the British government.
- Jameson launched a raid on the Transvaal, hoping to link up with discontented Uitlanders and to overthrow the Boer government. He and his followers were arrested, and the Uitlander rising did not take place.
- The Colonial Secretary, *Joseph Chamberlain,* was officially acquitted of the charge that he had known about the raid in advance, but this now seems unlikely to have been the truth.

■ *TIP* The episode worsened relations between Britain and the Boers, and was a long-term cause of the *Anglo–Boer War, 1899–1902.*

Jarrow March, 1936: the best known of several peaceful protests by unemployed people during the *Great Depression* of the 1930s.

- Jarrow is a town in industrial northeast England, where a large proportion of the population was dependent on employment in the shipbuilding industry.
- The march was a protest against serious job losses in the town. The marchers went to London to present their case for government intervention to provide employment.
- It was supported by both Conservative and Labour politicians in the area, although the most prominent figure was Ellen Wilkinson, the local Labour MP. Her book, *The Town That Was Murdered,* dealt with the problems of Jarrow.

■ *TIP* The march is a classic illustration of regional problems during the Great Depression.

Jenkins, Roy (1920–): Home Secretary 1965–67, 1974–76; Chancellor of the Exchequer 1967–70; deputy leader of the *Labour Party* 1970–72; a founder and first leader (1981–83) of the *Social Democratic Party (SDP).*

- As Home Secretary in *Wilson*'s first Labour government, Jenkins promoted liberal social reforms, such as laws on homosexuality and divorce. He was associated with the idea of the 'permissive society', in which older social conventions were relaxed.

- Jenkins was a pro-*EEC*, moderate/right-wing Labour figure, who was increasingly out of sympathy with the party's leftward drift. He spent the period 1976–80 out of British politics as President of the European Commission, the EEC's ruling body.
- On his return to British politics, he helped to found the Social Democratic Party and to guide it into alliance and eventual merger with the *Liberal Party*.
- He was a *Liberal Democrat* peer in the 1990s, associated with *Blair*, who appointed him to chair a commission on *proportional representation*.
- He is a historian and biographer of *Asquith, Baldwin* and *Gladstone*.

jingoism: an aggressive, self-confident patriotism.

- The term derives from a music hall song popular during an episode in the *Eastern Question* in 1877–78, when British naval forces were sent to protect Constantinople (now Istanbul, then the capital of the Turkish empire) against a possible Russian attack.
- The song went as follows: 'We don't want to fight, but by jingo if we do, we've got the ships, we've got the men, we've got the money too!'

Joseph, Sir Keith (1918–94): Health and Social Security Secretary 1970–74; Industry Secretary 1979–81; Education Secretary 1981–86.

- After serving in *Heath*'s Conservative government, Joseph became convinced that the *Conservative Party* had accepted too much of the *Labour Party*'s policy and outlook since 1945. He founded the Centre for Policy Studies, a *think tank* intended to move the Conservative Party back towards a more overtly free-market approach.
- He was a close associate of Margaret *Thatcher*, whom he influenced in the direction of *monetarism*. He was seen by some as a possible replacement for Heath as leader in 1974, but ruled himself out and supported Thatcher instead.
- He was an intellectual figure, unpopular for his uncompromising right-wing views, and of limited effectiveness as a minister.

Keynesian economics: ideas associated with the Cambridge economist John Maynard Keynes (1883–1946), who argued in the 1930s that governments could encourage recovery from a depression by investing in public works schemes.

- Keynes's major work was the ***General Theory of Employment, Interest and Money*** (1936). In it, he outlined the concept of the 'multiplier'. In a depression, governments should spend money on employment-creating schemes. This revives demand for manufactured goods and lifts the level of economic activity. To finance such a policy, he argued that government should run a deficit (allowing expenditure to exceed income).
- His theories were largely ignored by the governments of the 1930s, but enjoyed widespread support after 1945.
- From the mid-1970s, with the return of large-scale unemployment and *inflation*, there was growing doubt about Keynes's theories. Followers of the doctrine of *monetarism* criticised Keynesian ideas.
- The abandonment of Keynesian ideas began in response to the *International Monetary Fund (IMF)* crisis of 1976.

Khaki Election, 1900: the name given to the general election fought in the middle of the *Anglo–Boer War, 1899–1902*, which confirmed the *Conservative Party* under *Salisbury* in power.

- The Conservatives called an early election in September 1900, to exploit early successes in the Anglo–Boer War and divisions in the *Liberal Party* between supporters and opponents of the war.
- Colonial Secretary *Joseph Chamberlain* dominated the election campaign, labelling the Liberals as unpatriotic sympathisers with Britain's enemies.

Kilmainham Treaty, 1882: an agreement between *Gladstone* and *Parnell,* leader of the *Irish Nationalist Party*, that Parnell should be released from jail in return for calming disturbances in Ireland.

- Parnell was placed in Kilmainham Jail, Dublin, by the Liberal government in 1881, in the belief that he was associated with *Land League* violence in Ireland.
- When the disturbances did not subside, Gladstone decided to win Parnell's co-operation by releasing him, subject to certain conditions.

- The deal provoked the resignation of the Chief Secretary for Ireland, W. E. Forster, and the Lord Lieutenant (Viceroy), Lord Cowper, who had been kept in the dark by Gladstone.
- See also *Phoenix Park murders*.

Kinnock, Neil (1942–): leader of the *Labour Party* 1983–92; member of the European Commission since 1993.

- Kinnock came from the left of the Labour Party but dedicated himself after the disastrous 1983 general election to making the party electable, by ditching unpopular left-wing policies.
- Following his speech to the 1985 party conference, condemning the extremism of the *Militant Tendency*, he began removing hard-left activists from the party.
- He adopted modern media techniques and began changing the party's image, to the disgust of traditional socialists. He also commissioned a policy review in the late 1980s, which led to the abandonment of Labour's commitment to unilateral (one-sided) nuclear disarmament and ideas of having a state-run economy.
- In spite of changes, Labour failed to win the 1987 and 1992 general elections.

TIP Kinnock's period as Labour leader needs to be seen in longer perspective, in many ways preparing for the more fundamental changes made by *Blair* after 1994.

Kitchener, Horatio Herbert (Lord Kitchener of Khartoum) (1850–1916): a successful British general in the 1898 Sudanese campaign and *Anglo–Boer War, 1899–1902*; Secretary for War 1914–16.

- Kitchener conquered the Sudan for Britain in 1898, winning the victory of Omdurman. He also faced down the French challenge at Fashoda, thus securing British control of the Nile Valley. This was essential for the security of Egypt, ruled by Britain since 1882.
- He helped to win the Anglo–Boer War of 1899–1902 by a policy of blockhouses (fortified units linked by barbed wire) and by driving Boer civilians into concentration camps, thus depriving enemy guerrilla fighters of local support.
- He was appointed War Secretary by Asquith on the outbreak of the First World War.
- He was popular with the public (a well-known recruiting poster featured his face), but secretive and mistrustful of *Cabinet* colleagues.
- He was drowned on a mission to Russia when his ship hit a German mine off the Orkney Islands.

Kruger, Paul (1825–1904): President of the Transvaal Republic 1881–1900 and opponent of Britain in the *Anglo–Boer Wars* of 1881 and 1899–1902.

- Kruger came into conflict with Britain through his refusal to allow voting rights for foreign gold prospectors ('Uitlanders'), who had settled in the Transvaal since the 1880s.
- He saw Britain's support of the Uitlanders as a bid to win dominance in southern Africa. He wanted to maintain Boer control of his country.

- He received a famous telegram of congratulation from the German Kaiser William II in 1896, following his defeat of the *Jameson raid*. This worsened relations with Britain.
- He went to war with Britain in October 1899 following a breakdown of negotiations with the British, and fled abroad after the Transvaal was taken over by Britain in 1900.

Labour Party: a political party formed as the Labour Representation Committee (LRC) in February 1900, with the intention of improving the lives of working-class people through parliamentary action.

● It became known as the Labour Party in 1906. It was formed through an alliance of trade unions and socialists. The party formally adopted a commitment to nationalisation (state ownership of key sections of the economy) in *Clause Four* of its 1918 Constitution.

● It was in power as a minority government in 1924 and 1929–31. The first majority Labour government, led by *Attlee*, carried through important measures of nationalisation and laid the foundations of the *welfare state* (1945–51). It was in office again from 1964 to 1970, 1974 to 1979, and since 1997.

● The party's internal history has been affected by continual tension between cautious moderates and left-wingers who have wanted rapid social change. Labour's association with the trade unions has been a source of strength but has also opened the party to charges (especially in the 1970s) that it is dominated by a powerful interest group.

● The long period in opposition, from 1979 to 1997, persuaded Labour that it must change its image and policies in order to be electable once again. Under *Blair*, the idea of 'New Labour' has developed. The modern Labour Party accepts many of the free-market attitudes of the Conservatives and is more distant from the trade unions.

▨ *TIP* Exam questions on the Labour Party require a knowledge of the various groups which composed it, especially the trade unions.

Labour Representation Committee: see *Labour Party*.

laissez-faire: the belief, widely held in the nineteenth century, that government should intervene as little as possible in society and the economy.

● There was general agreement that government action, even if undertaken for the best of motives, could have damaging effects. Receiving government assistance would remove the incentive for individual effort and undermine people's sense of self-respect.

● This way of thinking helps to explain the *New Poor Law, 1834*, which aimed to discourage the poor from seeking help by making workhouses deliberately unattractive places.

- Nonetheless, it was accepted that exceptions would have to be made for certain categories of people, such as women and child factory workers.
- From the 1880s, the basis of laissez-faire was increasingly criticised as the persistence of large-scale social problems became apparent.
- *TIP* Be able to quote examples of laissez-faire in action in Victorian Britain, and examples of ways in which it was not strictly followed.

Land League: an organisation formed to protect Irish tenant farmers against their landlords in 1879.

- Ireland was hit by an agricultural depression in the mid-1870s and landlords responded by reorganising their estates and evicting tenants.
- The Land League was formed by Michael Davitt (1846–1906) to resist evictions. Members carried out attacks on landlords and their property (the 'Land War'). Tenants who took over farms from which people had been evicted were 'boycotted' (shunned by the local community). The name comes from Captain Boycott, a victim of this tactic.
- *TIP* The Land League is important for the study of *Gladstone* and Ireland.

Lansbury, George (1859–1940): editor of the Labour newspaper, the *Daily Herald*, 1919–22; First Commissioner of Works 1929–31; leader of the *Labour Party* 1931–35.

- Lansbury became leader of the Labour Party after the October 1931 electoral defeat removed virtually all of its senior figures from the *House of Commons*.
- He was popular with the party's rank and file for his sincerity but lacked political skill and governmental experience.
- He was an uncompromising pacifist who at the October 1935 party conference opposed any action against Italy's threatened invasion of Abyssinia. For this he was publicly attacked by *Bevin*, causing him to resign the leadership.

Lansdowne, Lord, Henry Petty-Fitzmaurice (1845–1927): Governor-General of Canada 1883–88; Viceroy of India 1888–94; War Secretary 1895–1900; Foreign Secretary 1900–05; Minister without Portfolio 1915–16.

- As Foreign Secretary, Lansdowne began a search for security through alliances or understandings with other powers. This has been seen by some historians as a significant break with the more detached attitude of *Salisbury*.
- He was responsible for the *Anglo–Japanese Alliance, 1902*, and the *Anglo–French Agreement, 1904*. He was not, however, fundamentally hostile to Germany and remained open to the idea of an Anglo–German agreement.
- He led the *Conservative Party* in the *House of Lords* in close co-operation with *Balfour*. He was also a key figure in the 1909–11 constitutional crisis culminating in the conflict over the *Parliament Act*. A leading Southern Irish landowner, he was a strong opponent of *Home Rule*.
- In 1917 Lansdowne appealed, via a public letter, for a negotiated end to the First World War, which he saw as a threat to the survival of civilisation.

■ TIP In answering questions on Lansdowne's foreign policy, show awareness of the elements of continuity with earlier policies, as well as the ways in which it marked a change.

Law, Andrew Bonar (1858–1923): leader of the *Conservative Party* 1911–21, 1922–23; Colonial Secretary 1915–16; Chancellor of the Exchequer 1916–19; Lord Privy Seal 1919–21; Prime Minister 1922–23.

- Law had an aggressive style as leader of the Conservative Party before the First World War, especially in opposition to the Liberal government's plans for Irish *Home Rule*.
- He was a member of *Lloyd George*'s War Cabinet and a vital support for the *coalition* government in both war and peace.
- He resigned because of poor health in March 1921, but was sufficiently recovered to return the following year to head the *Carlton Club revolt* against Lloyd George. He is credited with restoring the Conservative Party's identity as a party of government in its own right.
- His own premiership was cut short by the discovery that he was suffering from terminal cancer.

League of Nations: an organisation created after the First World War to provide a forum for the peaceful settlement of international disputes. It also tackled social problems such as disease and slavery.

- The League was the idea of Woodrow Wilson, President of the USA 1913–21, although he could not persuade his own country to join it. It was based in Geneva.
- In the 1920s and 1930s, many people in Britain put their faith in the League as a guarantee against another world war. The idea of 'collective security', whereby countries agreed to work together in the interests of peace, was popular. Many people joined the League of Nations Union, a pressure group that supported the League.
- The League had limited power to control aggressive countries such as Mussolini's Italy or Hitler's Germany. Economic sanctions (a refusal to trade with an aggressor country) proved ineffective against Italy in the *Abyssinian War, 1935–36*. This damaged the League's credibility.

Liberal Democrat Party: the outcome of a merger between the *Liberal Party* and the *Social Democratic Party* in 1988.

- The party retains many of the traditional policy positions of the twentieth-century Liberal Party. It gives a high priority to social welfare, especially education and health, and is committed to constitutional reform.
- Its pro-Europeanism and its support for Scottish and Welsh *devolution* have given it common ground with *Blair*'s *Labour Party*. After the 1997 general election, some Liberal Democrat MPs were invited to join a Labour *Cabinet* committee. Thus far it has been disappointed in its hope of *proportional representation*, even though a prominent Liberal Democrat peer, Lord *Jenkins*, was asked to report on the electoral system.

- The party was led by Paddy *Ashdown* from 1988 to 1999. He was succeeded by Charles Kennedy in 1999.

Liberal imperialist: a follower of Lord *Rosebery* in the 1890s and early 1900s, who wanted to see the *Liberal Party* adopt a more positive attitude towards the *British empire*.

- Liberal imperialists believed that the Liberal Party would continue to be excluded from power unless it re-examined its traditionally negative attitude towards imperial development. Some of them linked this to a positive view of state intervention to tackle social problems.

- They remained a minority of the party but had a well-funded organisation, the Liberal League. They included three key members of the 1905–15 Liberal governments, *Asquith, Grey* and *Haldane.*

- During the *Anglo–Boer War, 1899–1902,* their open disagreements with Liberal opponents of the war contributed to the party's continuing weakness.

Liberal National: a Liberal who followed Sir John Simon (1873–1954) in giving support to the Conservative-dominated *National Governments* of 1931–40.

- Liberal Nationals found common ground with the Conservatives in their readiness to tackle the *Great Depression* with public spending cuts and protective tariffs for British industry. They were rewarded with posts in the National Governments. Sir John Simon served as Foreign Secretary 1931–35, Home Secretary 1935–37 and Chancellor of the Exchequer 1937–40.

- After 1947, Liberal Nationals (who later became known as National Liberals) amalgamated with the Conservatives.

Liberal Party: a political party that evolved in the mid-nineteenth century and was committed to *free trade*, reform of national institutions and religious and political equality for people who did not belong to the established *Anglican Church*.

- The name 'Liberal' was used from the 1830s to denote a supporter of the *Franchise Act, 1832.* However, the formal creation of the Liberal Party has usually been dated to 1859, when a combination of *Whigs, Peelites* and *Radicals* came together in the Willis's Rooms meeting.

- The nineteenth-century party consisted of a variety of different viewpoints, and there was considerable disagreement about the pace of change. The issue of *Home Rule* for Ireland split the party in 1886 and put it out of power for most of the next 20 years.

- In the twentieth century, the party supported a more positive role for the state in promoting social welfare (*New Liberalism*).

- A division between followers of *Asquith* and *Lloyd George* during the First World War, combined with a long-term organisational decline, made the party an increasingly marginal force.

- Britain's electoral system, which favours parties whose voting strength is concentrated in certain constituencies, worked against the Liberals. Their calls for a reform of the system, to make the number of votes cast for a party more proportional to the number of seats won, have failed to make headway. Although — as in the early 1960s and again in the early 1970s — the party was capable of spectacular by-election wins, this did not translate into success at general elections.

- After 1981, the Liberal Party entered into an alliance with the *Social Democratic Party (SDP)* and in 1988 the two merged to form the *Liberal Democrat Party.*

■ *TIP* Exam questions on the Liberal Party, either in the nineteenth or twentieth centuries, require a clear definition of 'Liberal' in the context of the period.

Liberal Tory: a member of the *Tory Party* in the period 1815–30 who seemed to be sympathetic to political and economic change.

- Prominent 'Liberal Tories' included *Canning, Goderich, Huskisson* and *Peel.* They were in favour of *free trade* and other policies that made the Tory government of *Liverpool* more responsive to the demands of the middle classes.
- Nonetheless, the term 'Liberal Tory' is fraught with difficulty. Historians no longer accept, as was once argued, that there was a clear-cut division between two phases of Liverpool's government, around 1822. It was not the case that a repressive, negative period was succeeded by a more enlightened, open phase. 'Liberal Tories' served both before and after 1822. Historians now detect continuity of policy over the period of Tory government.
- Politicians are not easily 'pigeon-holed'. It was quite possible for someone like Peel to be a 'Liberal' supporter of free trade and of humanitarian changes to the legal and prison system, yet to be opposed to *Catholic emancipation.* Neither Peel nor Canning saw any reason to reform the electoral system, although Huskisson cautiously embraced this towards the end of his career.

■ *TIP* It is worth looking closely at government policies during the Liverpool era, to see how the ground was prepared for post-1822 'Liberal Tory' reforms in the pre-1822 period.

Liberal Unionist: a Liberal who left *Gladstone's Liberal Party* through opposition to *Home Rule* for Ireland.

- Most of the Liberal Unionist MPs were *Whigs* or moderates who feared the consequences of handing over Irish government to a nationalist movement associated with attacks on property and with hostility to the *British empire.*
- An important minority of Liberal Unionists consisted of *Radical* supporters of *Joseph Chamberlain.* They felt that their positive ideas for tackling social problems were being sidelined by Gladstone.
- Liberal Unionists supported the 1886–92 *Salisbury* government in Parliament and one of them, G. J. Goschen, accepted the post of Chancellor of the Exchequer. Several of them were given *Cabinet* posts in the 1895–1905 Conservative governments.
- The Liberal Unionist Party was formally amalgamated with the Conservatives in 1912.

Lib–Lab: a type of Liberal MP of working-class origin, elected to Parliament between the 1870s and the 1890s.

- Numbers of Lib–Lab MPs remained limited because until 1911 there were no salaries for MPs. If a candidate did not have a private income, his only hope was to secure sponsorship from a trade union or other organisation.
- Examples of Lib–Lab MPs included the miners' representative Thomas Burt, and the former stonemason Henry Broadhurst, who became the first working-class government minister (Under-Secretary at the Home Office) in 1886.
- In Parliament, Lib–Lab MPs generally accepted Liberal Party policies and did not try to develop a specifically working-class viewpoint.

Lib–Lab Pact, 1903: an agreement between the *Liberal Party* and the Labour Representation Committee (LRC). The Liberals agreed not to oppose Labour candidates in 50 constituencies, in return for Labour support for the Liberals in Parliament.

- The agreement was negotiated by Herbert Gladstone, the Liberal Chief Whip, and Ramsay *MacDonald*, secretary of the LRC.
- It suited the Liberals because, in the designated constituencies, they would have stood little chance of winning. The LRC also stood to gain because its organisation remained weak in many areas and Liberal opposition would have been a serious problem. Both parties recognised that in some seats (as at North East Lanark in 1901), a Liberal and a Labour candidate might split the vote between them and allow the Conservative to win.
- Labour won 29 seats in the 1906 general election, compared with only 2 in 1900.

▪ *TIP* The pact is important for the early growth of the body which became known as the *Labour Party*.

Lib–Lab Pact, 1977–78: an agreement by the *Liberal Party* under David Steel (leader 1976–88) to support *Callaghan*'s Labour government in Parliament.

- The Labour government needed support because it had lost a number of seats in by-elections. Both Labour and the Liberals wanted to prevent a Conservative victory in a vote in the *House of Commons*.
- Labour agreed to consult the Liberals and offered them a system of direct elections to the European Parliament and *devolution* for Scotland and Wales.
- The pact broke down when the government failed to deliver either *proportional representation* for European elections or devolution.

Lichfield House Compact, 1835: a meeting of *Whigs, Radicals* and Irish MPs loyal to *O'Connell,* who formed an alliance to unseat *Peel*'s Conservative government.

- Peel's 1834–35 government was in a minority in the *House of Commons* and it did not take long for the authors of the compact to find an opportunity to defeat him. He was replaced by a Whig government under *Melbourne.*
- The alliance was not a solid one. The Conservatives were able to exploit the fact that the Whigs had done a deal with the Irish Party, which they portrayed as a threat to British interests. Whigs and Radicals were unable to agree on the pace and scope of change.

Liverpool, Lord (Robert Banks Jenkinson) (1770–1828): Foreign Secretary

1801–04; Home Secretary 1804–06, 1807–09; Secretary for War and the Colonies 1809–12; Prime Minister 1812–27.

- Liverpool was the longest-serving Prime Minister of the nineteenth century, who held together a government of strong personalities, such as *Canning* and *Wellington.*
- He was accused by *Radicals* of a harsh and repressive attitude towards popular movements, especially before 1821–22.
- Historians used to argue that there was a major change in the character of the government and that it became more 'Liberal' in the 1820s. It is now generally felt that there was more continuity of policy over the government as a whole. Liverpool favoured measures of *free trade* but circumstances did not allow their introduction until the 1820s.
- He maintained the unity of the *Tory Party* by preventing the discussion of divisive issues such as *Catholic emancipation.* After his removal by a stroke in February 1827, open conflict broke out.
- **TIP** Be able to discuss Liverpool's skills as Prime Minister. He is now generally regarded as an underrated political leader.

Lloyd George, David (1863–1945): President of the Board of Trade 1905–08; Chancellor of the Exchequer 1908–15; Minister of Munitions 1915–16; War Secretary 1916; Prime Minister 1916–22.

- Lloyd George came from a Welsh *nonconformist* background and was originally associated with the left of the *Liberal Party*, opposing the *Anglo–Boer War, 1899–1902.*
- A social reformer in the 1905–15 Liberal governments, he was noted for his taxation of the wealthy in the *People's Budget, 1909.*
- In the First World War, he emerged as the minister most committed to organising the country for war, creating the Ministry of Munitions to speed up arms production.
- Lloyd George succeeded *Asquith* as Prime Minister in December 1916 with Conservative support, causing a split in the Liberal Party. He continued in office as head of a *coalition* after winning the 1918 general election.
- He handled a range of postwar problems, including industrial conflict and the events leading up to the *Anglo–Irish Treaty, 1921.*
- He was distrusted for his 'presidential' style as Prime Minister and was eventually rejected by the Conservatives in the October 1922 *Carlton Club revolt.* He never held office again.

London Dock Strike, 1889: a 5-week strike by dock workers, demanding (and eventually securing) a guaranteed wage of 6 pence per hour.

- The dockers were led by three socialists, Ben Tillett, John Burns and Tom Mann, in demanding a minimum wage of the 'docker's tanner'.
- The strike was orderly and well organised, with widespread support among other riverside trades. Financial support from Australian trade unionists enabled the strike to continue.

- The dockers won public sympathy, and the mediation of the Lord Mayor of London and of Cardinal Manning, head of the Catholic Church in England, helped them to win.
- As a result, a dock workers' union was created, which soon had 30,000 members. This was an important advance in the making of the *New Unionism* of unskilled and semi-skilled workers.

Lovett, William: see *Chartism.*

Luddism: a popular movement against the use of machines in the textile industry between 1811 and 1816.

- Luddites took their name from a mythical leader known as Ned Ludd. They broke up machinery that they claimed was putting textile workers out of a job. They were also angered by rising food prices and low wages.
- They were active in the Midlands and northern England. The main outbreaks of violence occurred in 1811–12.

Lyons v. Wilkins, 1899: an appeal court ruling that limited the right of unions to picket in support of a strike.

- Peaceful picketing was seen by trade unions as essential for the success of a strike. This involves standing outside one's workplace and persuading other workers not to go in.
- The right to picket had been granted, with conditions, by the *Conspiracy and Protection of Property Act, 1875*. It was now called into question by the law courts.
- This was part of a challenge by employers to trade unions in the 1890s. It helped to persuade some unions that they needed a separate *Labour Party* to represent them in Parliament.
- *TIP* The case was important for the formation of the Labour Representation Committee (the future Labour Party) in 1900.

Maastricht Treaty, 1992: a treaty that transformed the European Community into the European Union, with increased powers over foreign policy and other areas of policy making.

- Pro-European Conservatives welcomed the treaty because they believed that, with the ending of the *Cold War,* Britain needed to develop its European dimension in order to have a world role. They also argued that European trade was essential to the British economy.
- *Major* shared these views and signed up to the treaty. He secured an 'opt out' from two policies which, he believed, were not in Britain's interests. One was the development of a single European currency. The other was the 'Social Chapter', which promised to extend common European rules on employment law, social security and other matters.
- Nonetheless, the treaty caused concern among 'Euro-sceptics' in the *Cabinet* and the party. The debate on the treaty in Parliament was fiercely contested by opponents, who viewed Maastricht as an unacceptable limitation on Britain's freedom as an independent nation state.

MacDonald, James Ramsay (1866–1937): Labour Prime Minister January to October 1924, 1929–31; Prime Minister of the *National Government* 1931–35; Lord President of the Council 1935–37; leader of the *Labour Party* 1911–14, 1922–31.

- MacDonald played a key role in founding the Labour Representation Committee and in expanding its support through negotiations with trade unions after the *Taff Vale Case.* He negotiated the *Lib–Lab Pact, 1903.*
- An effective leader (known at that time as chairman) of the Parliamentary Labour Party, he resigned over his opposition to Britain's involvement in war in 1914.
- He led two minority Labour governments in 1924 and 1929–31. His priority was to avoid radical changes, which might disturb public opinion and cause the Labour movement to be seen as a dangerous revolutionary force.
- In the financial crisis of August 1931, he supported the spending cuts required by international bankers as the price of a loan. When the Labour government split over this proposal, MacDonald formed a National Government with the Conservatives and Liberals.

- He was expelled from the Labour Party for what was seen as a betrayal of the working-class movement. He became leader of a small group of ex-Labour MPs known as the National Labour Party. It took until the 1970s before a more balanced view of his actions could be taken.

Macleod, Iain (1913–70): Minister of Health 1952–55; Minister of Labour 1955–59; Colonial Secretary 1959–61; Chancellor of the Duchy of Lancaster and *Conservative Party* chairman 1961–63; Chancellor of the Exchequer 1970.

- Macleod was a liberal Conservative, best remembered for his work as Colonial Secretary. He accelerated Britain's withdrawal from its colonies in Africa, in the belief that this was necessary to avoid chaos and anti-Western feeling in those countries. For this he was hated by the Conservative right wing.

- He refused to serve in the government of *Douglas-Home* because he believed that the party should have chosen a leader from the *House of Commons*. He also attacked the 'magic circle' of upper-class Conservatives around *Macmillan*, whom he claimed had fixed the succession.

- He died 1 month after taking office as Chancellor in *Heath*'s government.

TIP Macleod is an important figure for the study of Britain and *decolonisation*.

Macmillan, Harold (Earl of Stockton) (1894–1986): Minister of Housing 1951–54; Minister of Defence 1954–55; Foreign Secretary 1955; Chancellor of the Exchequer 1955–57; Prime Minister and leader of the *Conservative Party* 1957–63.

- He was seen in the 1920s and 1930s as a progressive Conservative MP. Experience of unemployment, witnessed in his northern industrial constituency of Stockton, made him favour a *Keynesian* approach to economic depression.

- He owed his promotion in the 1950s to his opposition to *appeasement* and his wartime association with Churchill. He became Prime Minister following the ending of *Eden*'s career by the *Suez Crisis, 1956.*

- Macmillan associated the Conservative Party with the consumer affluence of the late 1950s, and won the 1959 general election. He speeded up Britain's withdrawal from empire in Africa, following his 1960 *'wind of change' speech* in Cape Town, and decided to make Britain's first application to join the *EEC*, which was rejected by France in 1963.

- His final months in office were hit by scandals, including the *Profumo affair.* These damaged his reputation as the unflappable 'Supermac'.

- In retirement, he criticised *Thatcher* for leading the party in an uncompromising free market direction.

Major, John (1943–): Foreign Secretary 1989; Chancellor of the Exchequer 1989–90; Prime Minister and leader of the *Conservative Party* 1990–97.

- Major received rapid promotion after many years of obscurity following his election to Parliament in 1979. He gained the premiership when *Thatcher* resigned, because it was believed that he was best placed to stop *Heseltine* and unite the Conservative Party. He was expected to present *Thatcherism* with a human face.

- He won the 1992 general election, but his leadership was soon called into question by Britain's departure from the *Exchange Rate Mechanism (ERM)* on Black Wednesday.
- He was unable to prevent the party from descent into conflict between rival factions over Britain's role in Europe. Constant attacks on his leadership led him to resign in 1995 and invite challengers. John Redwood, the right-wing Welsh Secretary, ran against Major, who narrowly won.
- In 1997, Major led the party to its largest election defeat since 1832.

Manchester School: see *Cobden*.

manhood suffrage: see *Chartism*.

Maynooth affair, 1845: a controversy over the funding of Maynooth College, Ireland's leading seminary for the training of Catholic priests, which caused difficulty for *Peel*'s government.

- Peel proposed an increase in the annual government grant to Maynooth College, near Dublin. His idea was to influence the Catholic clergy, who were powerful opinion formers, in the direction of support for Britain's connection with Ireland.
- The proposal caused controversy with right-wing *Ultras* in the *Conservative Party*, who regarded Peel as unsound on the defence of Protestant rule in Ireland. The bill to increase the grant was passed, but 149 Conservative MPs voted against it.

■ *TIP* The affair was an important episode in the events leading to Peel's eventual rejection by a large number of Conservative MPs in 1846.

means test: an assessment of an unemployed person's income by the authorities in interwar Britain, in order to gauge entitlement to unemployment benefit.

- Introduced by the *National Government* in 1931 as part of its cost-cutting efforts to deal with the financial crisis, the means test was administered by the local authority Public Assistance Committees (PACs). It continued until 1941.
- The test was deeply unpopular with working-class families because the PACs were staffed by officials who had been connected with the hated *New Poor Law* system. The investigators pried into household details, sometimes recommending the sale of items of furniture. Benefit could be reduced if a member of the unemployed person's family had some earnings. Resentment of the test played a part in moving public opinion towards support for the *Labour Party* prior to the 1945 general election.

Mediterranean Agreements, 1887: two agreements between Britain, Italy and Austria, designed to maintain the *balance of power* in the Mediterranean region.

- The first agreement, between Britain and Italy, was intended to prevent France from gaining too much power in the Mediterranean and North Africa. The second, between Britain, Italy and Austria, was directed against Russian expansion in the area bordering the Black Sea and the Straits of Constantinople. The three powers agreed to co-operate to prevent unwelcome change.

- These agreements reflected the wish of the British government, under *Salisbury*, to uphold its interests in particular situations by means of specific, limited agreements. Salisbury preferred this to the signature of formally binding treaties. The agreements took the form of an exchange of notes between the various powers involved.

- The agreements were discontinued in 1896 because Britain could not agree to Austrian proposals for a definite military commitment to the defence of Constantinople against the Russians.

- **TIP** The agreements demonstrate the fact that Britain did not deliberately choose a policy of *splendid isolation* in the nineteenth century. Britain was prepared to conclude agreements with other powers where its interests were concerned.

Melbourne, Lord (William Lamb) (1779–1848): Chief Secretary for Ireland 1827–28; Home Secretary 1830–34; Prime Minister 1834, 1835–41.

- Melbourne's early career was as a *Liberal Tory*, resigning from *Wellington*'s government in 1828 with *Huskisson*. He joined *Grey*'s *Whig* government in 1830, having accepted the idea of parliamentary reform.

- He was a tough Home Secretary who repressed the *Captain Swing* rioters and the *Tolpuddle Martyrs*.

- He was briefly Prime Minister in 1834 before being dismissed by King William IV in a dispute over Irish Church reform. He was the last Prime Minister to be dismissed.

- As Prime Minister from 1835–41, Melbourne presided over several important reforms, including the *Municipal Corporations Act, 1835*, civil registration of births, marriages and deaths, and a law to allow *nonconformists* and Catholics to marry in their own churches.

- He was friend and adviser to the young Queen *Victoria*, and was her first Prime Minister.

- He was defeated by the Conservatives in the 1841 general election; this was the first time that a government was turned out by the voters rather than by King or Parliament.

- **TIP** You should be able to assess the significance of the reforms of the Melbourne government. Some historians have argued that they amount to an administrative revolution.

Midlothian campaigns, 1879–80: two public-speaking tours by *Gladstone* of Midlothian, a lowland Scottish constituency, during which he attacked the policies of the Conservative government.

- These were the first examples of a public-speaking campaign by a former Prime Minister. Gladstone had retired from Parliament in 1875 but had returned to politics to attack the imperial policies of *Disraeli*'s government.

- Gladstone was seeking to win the Midlothian seat, but it provided a platform for a national campaign. The recent reverses in the *Afghan Wars, 1878–79* and the *Zulu War, 1879* gave him an opportunity for this. He attacked government policies as an immoral and wasteful interference with the rights of small nations.

- The campaigns played a part in the Liberal victory in the 1880 general election.

Militant Tendency (Revolutionary Socialist League)**:** a far-left organisation within the *Labour Party*, prominent in the early 1980s, which tried to take over constituency Labour parties.

- Members were Trotskyist revolutionaries who followed the teachings of Russian Marxist Leon Trotsky (1879–1940). They believed in penetrating working-class organisations and capturing them for their own ends. Their most spectacular success was in Liverpool, where militants controlled the City Council.
- It is possible that their numbers and real influence have been exaggerated, but they damaged the Labour Party's image by suggesting that it was moving to the extreme left.
- *Kinnock* attacked Militant Tendency in a famous party conference speech in 1985 and expelled its members from the Labour Party.
- **TIP** This action was an essential part of the changes in the Labour Party in the late 1980s and 1990s, which eventually made it electable again.

Mill, John Stuart (1806–73): a leading philosopher whose key work, *On Liberty* (1859), became a text of the nineteenth-century *Liberal Party*.

- Mill argued that people should be free to act as they choose, provided their actions do not interfere with the liberty of others. This balance between freedom and law was central to nineteenth-century Liberalism.
- He was a Liberal MP from 1865 to 1868. He supported votes for women and tried to have this demand included in the *Franchise Act, 1867.*

Milner, Sir Alfred (Lord Milner) (1854–1925): British High Commissioner in Cape Colony, southern Africa 1897–1905; member of the *Lloyd George* War Cabinet 1916–18; War Secretary 1918; Colonial Secretary 1919–21.

- Milner was a committed imperialist who distrusted democracy and party politics, which he saw as obstacles to the national interest.
- As Britain's representative in South Africa, he conducted negotiations with the Boer leaders. He has been held responsible by some historians for the *Anglo–Boer War, 1899–1902.*
- His decision to import Chinese labourers to work in the South African gold mines after the war created the scare about *Chinese slavery*, which helped to lose the Conservatives the 1906 election.
- On his return to Britain, he confirmed his reputation as a hard-line imperialist and opponent of Liberal policies.
- During the First World War, he served as a member of Lloyd George's small War Cabinet, formed to run the war more effectively.

minority government: a government that tries to govern without an overall majority of seats in the *House of Commons.*

- Such a government does not form a *coalition*, but needs the support of another party or parties from the outside. Examples include the Labour governments

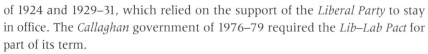

of 1924 and 1929–31, which relied on the support of the *Liberal Party* to stay in office. The *Callaghan* government of 1976–79 required the *Lib–Lab Pact* for part of its term.

mixed economy: the post-1945 idea that there should be a balance between state ownership of certain key industries and services and a continuing role for the private sector.

● This idea was at the heart of the notion of a *postwar consensus* between the *Labour* and *Conservative parties*. Conservative governments broadly accepted the *nationalisation* measures of the *Attlee* government of 1945–51, and later Labour governments accepted that large parts of the economy were better left in private hands.

● This idea was challenged after 1979, when the *Thatcher* government began a programme of *privatisation*.

Mond–Turner talks, 1928–29: discussions between Sir Alfred Mond, head of Imperial Chemical Industries (ICI) and Ben Turner, chairman of the *Trades Union Congress (TUC)* General Council, on improving the efficiency of industry.

● The talks reflected the more moderate, pragmatic approach of trade unions to industrial relations after the failure of the *General Strike*.

● They were an early example of corporatism — an attempt to bring together employers and unions to discuss matters of joint concern.

monetarism: an economic theory, developed by Milton Friedman and others in the 1950s, which stresses the importance of strict government control of the money supply.

● Monetarists criticised *Keynesian economics* for causing *inflation*. They argued that governments could squeeze out inflation by controlling the quantity of money in circulation. Rising unemployment was a price worth paying for the restoration of stable financial values.

● Monetarism influenced Sir Keith *Joseph* and, through him, Margaret *Thatcher* from the mid-1970s.

Montagu–Chelmsford reforms: see *Government of India Act, 1919*.

Morley–Minto reforms, 1909: measures to give Indians a greater role in the local administration of their own country, in order to make them more likely to accept British rule.

● The reforms were the work of John Morley, India Secretary 1905–10, and of Lord Minto, the Viceroy (representative of the British Crown in India).

● They gave Indians more representation on the provincial legislative (law-making) councils, which were concerned with local affairs. Elected Indians formed a majority of the membership of these councils.

● Some Indians were appointed to the Viceroy's executive council and to the all-India legislative council.

● The reforms ensured that Indian opinion was consulted to a greater extent, but did not give Indians real power.

Morrison, Herbert (1888–1965): Minister of Transport 1929–31; Minister of

Supply 1940; Home Secretary 1940–45; Lord President of the Council 1945–51; Foreign Secretary 1951; deputy leader of the *Labour Party* 1951–55.

- Morrison was organiser of the Labour Party in London and chief electoral strategist for the party at national level.
- He was on the right of the party, committed to making Labour a viable party of government.
- As business manager in the postwar Labour government, he was responsible for getting the programme of *nationalisation* and welfare reforms through Parliament.
- He was a supporter of 'consolidation' in the 1950s — building on the achievements of 1945–51 and demonstrating the party's competence, rather than forging ahead with radical new changes.

Mosley, Sir Oswald (1896–1980): Chancellor of the Duchy of Lancaster 1929–30; founded the New Party in 1931 and the British Union of Fascists (BUF) in 1932.

- Mosley began as a Conservative MP before switching to Labour and serving in the second *MacDonald* government.
- He resigned in 1930 after the rejection of his proposals for tackling unemployment through a programme of loan-financed public works and other radical measures.
- After founding the New Party, he started the British Union of Fascists, closely modelled on Mussolini's Blackshirts in Italy.
- The BUF stood for a combination of British nationalism, anti-Semitism and the creation of a dictatorship. It became involved in violent confrontations, especially in the East End of London (the 'Battle of Cable Street').
- The party never won mass support in Britain, partly because the violence and theatrical copying of foreign fascists offended people's sense of decency. Also, the impact of the *Great Depression* was never as universal as in Germany, and did not affect the economy in the early 1930s with the same suddenness. There was therefore less reason to support extreme solutions.
- The 1936 Public Order Act limited the BUF's activities by banning the wearing of political uniforms.
- After the Second World War, Mosley tried in vain to revive his political career by leading a movement opposed to *New Commonwealth* immigration.

■ *TIP* It is important to know why the extreme right represented by Mosley attracted so little support in the 1930s.

Mountbatten, Admiral of the Fleet Lord Louis (1900–79): Supreme Allied Commander in Southeast Asia 1943–45; last Viceroy of India 1947; First Sea Lord 1955–59; Chief of the Defence Staff 1959–65.

- Mountbatten was a member of the royal family (uncle of the Duke of Edinburgh) and a sailor by professional background.
- As Supreme Allied Commander in Southeast Asia, he contributed to the defeat of Japan in the Second World War.

- He was appointed Viceroy of India to oversee Britain's withdrawal. He negotiated with Nehru, leader of the Hindu Congress Party, and Jinnah, leader of the Muslim League, to arrange the partition of the subcontinent. Two states, Hindu-dominated India and Muslim-dominated Pakistan, emerged.
- As Chief of the Defence Staff, Mountbatten guided the unification of the three armed services under a new Ministry of Defence from 1964.
- He was assassinated by the *IRA* in 1979 while sailing off the Irish coast.

Munich Agreement, 1938: the classic example of *appeasement* in action, when Britain and France agreed to hand over the Sudetenland (the German-speaking part of Czechoslovakia) to Hitler's Germany.

- The agreement was approved by the majority of the British public, since there had been widespread fears of war with Germany in September 1938.
- Britain's Prime Minister, *Neville Chamberlain*, was accused of having been tricked by Hitler when, in March 1939, German troops took over the non-German part of Czechoslovakia. Britain then issued guarantees of support to Poland and other likely targets of German aggression.
- The Munich Agreement discredited appeasement, although its defenders have argued that it provided valuable time for rearmament.
- *TIP* Be able to describe and analyse the main arguments for and against the Munich Agreement.

Municipal Corporations Act, 1835: an act of the *Whig* government of *Melbourne* that created a system of borough (town) councils elected by ratepayers.

- The act tackled the problem of corrupt, self-appointed town councils that had not been representative of local people.
- All ratepayers (payers of local taxation) were allowed to vote. One third of the councillors were to be elected every year, to ensure accountability to the voters.
- Councils were given powers to deal with social issues such as public health if they chose to do so.
- The reform reflected the influence of *Benthamism* on the Whig government.
- *TIP* The act is an important feature of the reforms passed by the Whig governments of 1830–41.

Murdoch press: newspapers controlled by Rupert Murdoch (1931–), an Australian-born entrepreneur, owner of the News International company, associated with a popular style of presentation.

- In the early 1970s, Murdoch gained control of the ***Sun***, which became Britain's best-selling newspaper. Its emphasis on sensational stories and sport and its use of glamour photographs was imitated by other papers. Murdoch later bought ***The Times***.
- Murdoch started Sky Television, a satellite television station, in 1989. This became a major competitor of the BBC, especially in the area of sports broadcasting.

Nanking, Treaty of, 1842: see *Opium Wars*.

Napoleonic Wars, 1803–15: a continuation of the struggle waged by Britain and its continental European allies (Austria, Prussia, Russia) against the spread of the *French Revolution* after 1793.

● Britain fought to prevent the domination of Europe by the French leader, Napoleon Bonaparte. Until 1812, he was invariably victorious in battle on the continent. Britain's strength lay in its supremacy at sea, demonstrated by Admiral Nelson's victory at Trafalgar in 1805.

● On land, Britain's main involvement was in the Peninsular War (1808–13), which was fought to drive the French out of Spain and Portugal. Napoleon was forced to flee from France in 1814, but returned in 1815 for the '100 days' campaign. Britain's leading general in the Peninsular War, *Wellington*, went on to defeat Napoleon in the final battle of the war at Waterloo in 1815.

national efficiency: a belief, held by a number of politicians and others in the 1890s and early 1900s, that Britain's institutions needed thorough reform if the country was to continue as a *Great Power*.

● The belief was stimulated by Britain's poor performance in the *Anglo–Boer War, 1899–1902*. The physical unfitness of many recruits to the Army focused attention on the persistence of urban poverty and malnutrition.

● National efficiency enthusiasts were also worried about the need to improve technical education, the co-ordination of defence planning and other issues. In their minds, national strength and the quality of the population were closely interlinked.

● These ideas commanded support in sections of all three main political parties — among some Conservatives, *Liberal imperialists* and members of the *Fabian Society*.

● Reforms such as the *Education Act, 1902* and the provision of free school meals for poor children in 1906 were responses to national efficiency concerns.

▇ *TIP* National efficiency is important as background to the social reforms of the Liberal governments of 1905–14. It is linked to the growth of *New Liberalism*.

National Executive Committee (NEC): the governing body of the *Labour Party*, composed of delegates elected from the trade unions, the parliamentary party (the MPs) and the local constituency parties.

- The NEC is responsible for party administration at all levels, for party finance, election organisation and the selection of parliamentary candidates, together with policy research.

- Until the 1970s, it caused few problems for the party leaders, who could usually rely on the trade union component of the NEC to take a moderate line. In the *Wilson* era, however, the left wing gained influence and pushed through its own policy proposals, such as an extension of *nationalisation*. The NEC approved the left-wing manifesto on which the party fought and lost the 1983 general election.

- As part of the modernisation undertaken in the *Kinnock–Blair* era, the NEC was brought more under the control of the party leader.

National Government: the *coalition* governments that ran Britain between 1931 and 1940, which consisted of Conservatives and former members of the *Labour* and *Liberal parties* (National Labour and *Liberal Nationals*).

- The Prime Ministers were *MacDonald* from 1931 to 1935, *Baldwin* from 1935 to 1937 and *Neville Chamberlain* from 1937 to 1940.

- The first National Government was formed in August 1931 to deal with the financial crisis that destroyed the unity of the 1929–31 Labour government. It was originally expected to be a temporary arrangement, but the parties fought the 1931 general election together and won a large majority.

- The National Governments were opposed by the Labour Party and (from 1932) by Liberals under Sir Herbert Samuel, who resigned in protest at the abandonment of *free trade*.

TIP Know the reasons for the National Governments' domination of politics in the 1930s.

National Health Service (NHS): formed in 1948 by Labour minister *Bevan* to provide universal, free health care for the whole population.

- The hospital system was taken into public control and was to be administered through a series of regional boards. Health centres were to be built and medical provision was to be freely available.

- Bevan clashed with the doctors' pressure group, the British Medical Association (BMA), which feared that he was trying to turn doctors into salaried servants at the mercy of the state. Previously, doctors had been free to make money from private practices. To pacify the doctors, Bevan allowed them to continue treating private patients in NHS hospitals and assured them that a salary structure would not be imposed.

- The NHS proved to be more costly to run than expected, and in 1951 the Labour government imposed charges for false teeth and spectacles. Charges were later imposed for prescriptions.

- The cost of the NHS has continued to be a major political issue, although all parties have stated their support for the principle of a free service. The *Thatcher* government began a review of health-service financing in the late 1980s, and attempted to improve NHS efficiency by introducing private-sector ideas of management and competition. This led to hospitals taking responsibility for buying in services such as cleaning ('contracting out'), and to doctors running their own budgets ('GP fundholding').

- Concern about long hospital waiting lists was an important issue during and after the 1997 general election. The Labour government announced a major plan for reform and overhaul of the NHS in 2000.

National Insurance: a scheme introduced in 1911 and extended during the rest of the twentieth century, whereby employees make contributions to a common fund to insure themselves against ill health and unemployment.

- National Insurance was the work of the *Asquith* government and was based on schemes operated in Germany since the 1880s. The idea was that the employee, the employer and the government each made a weekly contribution, in order to build up a fund from which the worker could draw benefit in time of need.
- The health insurance scheme covered workers who earned less than £160 each year, and benefit could be drawn for 26 weeks. The worker's family was not covered. The unemployment scheme originally covered only workers in certain trades that were particularly vulnerable, such as building and shipbuilding, and benefit was restricted to 15 weeks in a year.
- National Insurance provision was extended to more workers during the interwar period. A comprehensive scheme for the whole working population was introduced by the *Attlee* government in 1946.

nationalisation: common or state ownership of key industries and services, which became official *Labour Party* policy in *Clause Four* of its 1918 constitution.

- Nationalisation of the coal industry was a long-standing demand of the miners' union. It was believed that it would make the industry more efficient and ensure that it was run more fairly from the workers' point of view. Like the railways, coal was making losses by the 1940s.
- The *Attlee* government nationalised the Bank of England and civil aviation in 1946; coal and cable and wireless in 1947; road haulage, railways and electricity in 1948; gas in 1949; and iron and steel in 1951.
- The Conservatives de-nationalised road haulage and steel (returned them to the private sector) after returning to office in 1951. This was because these industries had done well in private hands. Steel was re-nationalised by the Labour government of 1964–70.
- There was general agreement between the parties on state ownership until the election of the *Thatcher* government and its programme of *privatisation* after 1979.
- *TIP* Always be careful to define nationalisation clearly. In Britain, it meant government ownership and not workers' management of industry.

National Liberal Federation (NLF): an organisation created by *Joseph Chamberlain* in 1877 to represent the local Liberal Associations throughout Britain and to drive the *Liberal Party* towards more radical policies.

- By the 1870s, most large centres of population had their own local Liberal organisations. The purpose of the NLF was to draw them together and to put radical policies on the party's agenda at national level. It was intended to counteract the influence of the *Whigs*, who had acted as a force for moderation.
- Although *Gladstone* attended the opening meeting, the NLF was primarily a tool of Chamberlain and was based in his home city, Birmingham.
- After the Liberal Party split over Irish *Home Rule* in 1886, the NLF rebelled against Chamberlain and relocated to London. It remained a vehicle for radical policy proposals and hosted annual conferences, including the one at which the *Newcastle Programme* was adopted in 1891.

NATO: see *North Atlantic Treaty Organisation*.

Naval Defence Act, 1889: an act to expand the size of the Royal Navy to a two-power standard, so that it would be a match for the next two largest navies in the world combined.

- The act underlines the importance of the Navy in the nineteenth century for defending not only Britain's coastline, but also its overseas empire and trade routes. There were periodic public scares about national defence in the late Victorian period.
- It was directed against the French and Russians, who had moved closer together diplomatically and had begun to expand their navies. It allocated £21.5 million for naval spending.
- Although it led to a significant building programme, in 1893 the next government had to announce a further expansion, known as the Spencer Programme after Earl Spencer, the First Lord of the Admiralty (the minister responsible for the Navy).

NEC: see *National Executive Committee*.

Newcastle Programme, 1891: a set of policies adopted by *Gladstone* as *Liberal Party* leader at the Newcastle conference of the *National Liberal Federation*.

- Gladstone's acceptance of a range of policy proposals indicated his reliance on the *Radical* wing of his party after the *Home Rule* split of 1886 put the Liberals out of power. Many of the policies were adopted in response to pressure from interest groups within the party, and were not proposals with which Gladstone had much personal sympathy. This was the price he paid for having Home Rule as the party's first priority.
- The programme included the *disestablishment* of the Welsh and Scottish churches, votes for all men, taxation of land, the establishment of district and parish councils, and compulsory powers for local authorities to purchase land. Few of these were achieved after the Liberals won the 1892 general election, because the new government's dependence on Irish Nationalist votes meant that the attempt to pass Home Rule came first.

New Commonwealth: Commonwealth countries that either remained depend-encies of Britain or gained their independence from Britain after the Second World War.

- In the 1950s and 1960s, there was growing concern about the increasing number of immigrants from New Commonwealth countries, such as India, Pakistan and the West Indies. Some were recruited for specific purposes (for example, West Indians to work on London Transport) but most came inde-pendently, to seek a better life for their families.
- Immigrants faced discrimination in jobs and housing, encountering hostility in some white working-class urban areas where they settled.
- The 1962 Commonwealth Immigrants Act was a response to pressure for limitations on the entry of people from the New Commonwealth.

New Departure, 1879: the name given to the new and more determined strategy pursued by Irish nationalists who wanted *Home Rule* for their country.

- It involved the coming together of *Parnell* (soon to become leader of the *Irish Nationalist Party* in Parliament) with Michael Davitt, leader of the *Land League*. Parnell took up the call of tenant farmers for lower rents and an end to evictions.
- The background to this strategy was the onset of agricultural depression in Ireland, which had worsened the economic position of the tenants.
- Funding for the strategy was supplied by Clan Na Gael, an Irish-American organisation under John Devoy.
- It was crucial to the emergence of Parnell as the most powerful figure in Irish nationalism in the 1880s.

New Labour: see *Blair.*

New Liberalism: a change in the philosophy of the *Liberal Party* in the 1890s and 1900s, to embrace a more positive role for the state in tackling social problems.

- *Gladstonian Liberalism* in the nineteenth century had advocated a limited role for the state, so that individuals took responsibility for their own lives. The persistence of poverty in the late nineteenth century, and the fact that much of it was due to factors beyond the control of individuals, led to a change in the outlook of some Liberal thinkers.
- Intellectuals such as T. H. Green, L. T. Hobhouse and J. A. Hobson argued a case for government action to ensure a national minimum standard of living. Individuals could not be truly free unless liberated from the poverty that came from unemployment, sickness, old age and other factors. The graduated taxation of wealth would be the way to ensure a fairer distribution of resources. They argued that this was a development from Old Liberalism, and not a rejection of it.
- New Liberalism found practical expression in the reforms of the 1905–15 Liberal governments, such as *old age pensions* and *National Insurance*.

■ *TIP* It is worth knowing the similarities and differences between Old and New

Liberalism. Were they seeking the same ends but with different methods, or were they fundamentally different?

New Model Unions (also called 'craft unions'): trade unions that represented skilled workers in the nineteenth century.

- Skilled workers such as engineers organised themselves into unions in the mid-nineteenth century, earlier than unskilled and semi-skilled workers. They maintained high subscriptions and offered their members benefits such as pensions and funeral expenses. They were more concerned to protect their own privileges and to uphold their own rules and procedures than to seek fundamental changes in society.
- Members of New Model Unions tended to be Liberal supporters who gained the vote from the *Franchise Act, 1867*. They looked to the Liberals to secure for them the legal recognition that they lacked. The insecurity of their legal position was highlighted by the case of *Hornby v. Close, 1867*.
- They gained legal recognition in 1871 and the right of peaceful picketing in 1875.

New Poor Law, 1834 (also known as the 'Poor Law Amendment Act'): reform of the system under which the poor had been cared for since the Elizabethan period, intended to make it cheaper and more efficient.

- The new law was a response to criticisms that the *Old Poor Law* was too costly for property owners who had to pay for it, and that there were too many local variations in how poor relief was administered.
- Parishes were instructed to combine into groups known as unions, and each union was to build a workhouse. In order to receive assistance, an able-bodied person would have to submit to the 'workhouse test', giving up his or her independence and entering the workhouse. Each union was to be run by a board of guardians elected by local property owners. At national level, the system would be supervised by a Poor Law Commission based in London.
- The system worked on the principle of 'less eligibility' — conditions in the workhouse were to be less attractive than those of the lowest-paid independent worker. Inmates had to wear a uniform and carry out menial tasks, and families were separated.
- In industrial areas, where employment was subject to swings of the trade cycle, the workhouses could not cope in times of severe hardship. In these areas, the authorities had to continue dispensing financial assistance to people in their own homes (outdoor relief).
- The Poor Law Commission was replaced by a Poor Law Board after the *Andover workhouse scandal, 1846*. This was superseded by the Local Government Board in 1871.
- In 1929, responsibility for the workhouse system was transferred from the boards of guardians to local councils. By this time, most workhouses had changed in character and had turned into old people's homes or hospitals for the poor. The system was finally abolished in 1948.

■ *TIP* The New Poor Law was the most important of the *Whig* government reforms of 1833–41 and reflected the influence of *Benthamism* on policy makers.

Newport Rising, 1839: a protest by followers of *Chartism* in South Wales, after the rejection of the first Chartist petition by Parliament.

- South Wales was an area of rapid industrial growth (coal and iron and steel) and poor working-class living and working conditions were a factor in the protest.
- A demonstration at Newport became violent, and troops fired on the protestors. The leader, John Frost, was punished by being transported to Australia.
- This was an example of 'physical force Chartism'. It also demonstrated the ability of the authorities to suppress the movement.

New Unionism: the creation of unions by unskilled and semi-skilled workers in the late 1880s and early 1890s.

- These unions included the dockers and gas workers. They tended to be low paid and thus were not able to afford large subscriptions. Money paid into union funds was generally used to sustain strikes rather than to provide benefits.
- Many of the 'new union' leaders were socialists, such as Will Thorne (organiser of the gas workers), who wanted state action to promote greater social equality. The formation of these unions was associated with several major strikes over pay and conditions, such as the *London Dock Strike, 1889*.
- Trade union membership doubled in the period 1889–91. In the 1890s, it provoked a backlash by employers, who organised to resist union demands and to discipline workers.

NHS: see *National Health Service*.

Night of the Long Knives, 1962: the sacking by Prime Minister *Macmillan* of one third of his *Cabinet*, including the Chancellor of the Exchequer, Selwyn Lloyd.

- Macmillan's motives are not clear. He may have been seeking to change the image of the government following a period of declining popularity. Another version is that he was convinced that there was a plot against him.
- The move backfired because it seemed like a panic-stricken exercise of the Prime Minister's power to sack colleagues. It contributed to the declining fortunes of the Conservatives in the early 1960s.

NLF: see *National Liberal Federation*.

nonconformist: a member of one of the Protestant Churches other than the *Anglican Church*.

- Examples of nonconformist Churches include the Methodists, Baptists and Quakers.
- Nonconformists were the backbone of the nineteenth-century *Liberal Party*'s local support. They provided most of the membership of moral pressure groups such as the United Kingdom Alliance, which campaigned for temperance (restrictions on the alcoholic drink trade).

- They sought political and civil equality with the Church of England — for example, in the right to hold teaching posts at Oxford and Cambridge universities, which were monopolised by Anglicans until 1871. Some nonconformists wanted the disestablishment of the Anglican Church, so that all religions would be fully equal before the law. They formed the Liberation Society to press for this.
- Nonconformists responded to *Gladstone*'s style of leadership, which involved fighting for abstract moral issues rather than everyday 'bread-and-butter' questions.
- The political influence of nonconformity declined with falling numbers and the growth of a more materialistic approach to politics in the twentieth century.

North Atlantic Treaty Organisation (NATO): a Western alliance system created in 1949, which has been dominated militarily and economically by the USA.

- The alliance was formed in response to the growing threat posed by the Soviet Union in the early years of the *Cold War*. Britain joined as a result of Foreign Secretary *Bevin*'s determination to involve the USA in the defence of western Europe.
- NATO was ranged against the corresponding Soviet-dominated military alliance, the Warsaw Pact (created in 1955). Its main role was to deter a Soviet invasion of western Europe. All members agreed that they would treat an attack on one country as an attack on all.
- It did not take part in actual fighting during the Cold War. Its first military engagement came after the end of the Cold War, in the 1999 war to stop Serbia from dominating Kosovo.

Northcliffe, Lord (Alfred Harmsworth) (1865–1922): a newspaper owner who created modern popular journalism.

- In 1896, Northcliffe founded the ***Daily Mail***, which became the largest mass-circulation newspaper. It had a lively style, focusing on sensational and 'human interest' stories as well as providing political comment. He covered sporting events in greater detail than political speeches. Northcliffe also founded the ***Daily Mirror*** and gained control of ***The Times***, which he turned into a profitable enterprise.
- He worked for the government on propaganda during the First World War and tried to gain political influence with *Lloyd George*. He led a mission to the USA which played a part in that country's entry into the First World War.
- His main importance lies in the example he set for the owners of other popular papers. He put the wishes of the reader first and was determined that his papers would sell.
- *TIP* Northcliffe was a vital figure in the development of mass news media in the late nineteenth and early twentieth centuries.

Oastler, Richard (1789–1861): the organiser of the movement to limit the working hours of textile factory operatives, and a campaigner against the *New Poor Law* in the 1830s.

- Oastler was a Yorkshire land agent who saw the *Industrial Revolution* and accompanying political and social changes as a threat to traditional patterns of life. He was a Tory paternalist who believed that the rich and powerful had an obligation to care for the disadvantaged and, in return, a right to their obedience.
- He was a powerful writer, speaker and organiser. His 1830 letter on 'Yorkshire slavery', condemning the long hours and poor conditions of mill workers, started the campaign for *Factory Acts* to protect the victims of industrialisation.
- He opposed the New Poor Law because he saw the workhouse system as inhumane and an interference with historic local methods of treating poverty.
- His influence declined after 1840, when he fell into debt.

O'Connell, Daniel (1775–1847): an Irish nationalist leader and champion of Catholic rights, known as 'the Liberator'.

- O'Connell was an Irish lawyer and landowner who formed the Catholic Association in 1823 to campaign for *Catholic emancipation*. His election as MP for County Clare in 1828 forced the British government to grant emancipation.
- He created the Irish Party at Westminster, which joined with the *Whigs* and *Radicals* in the *Lichfield House Compact, 1835*, to remove *Peel*'s Conservative government from office. Afterwards, he supported the Whig government of 1835–41.
- In the 1840s, he campaigned for repeal of the *Act of Union*. Essentially a moderate, he called off a mass meeting at Clontarf in 1843 when the authorities banned it.
- He was arrested in 1844 and convicted for political offences. The verdict was overturned on appeal to the *House of Lords*.

O'Connor, Feargus (1794–1855): a *Radical* politician, best known for his involvement with *Chartism* in the 1830s and 1840s.

- O'Connor was MP for Cork from 1832 to 1835, and became involved with Chartism through his support for the protest movement against the *New Poor Law*.

O

- He was a powerful speaker and publicist who ran the leading Chartist newspaper, the **Northern Star**, from 1837. He was the main advocate of 'physical force Chartism' and played a part in causing the *Newport Rising, 1839.*
- In 1846, he formed the National Land Company to settle Chartists in farming colonies. This was an attempt to cope with unemployment and to give working people self-respect. However, it was poorly thought out and was a financial failure.
- O'Connor became MP for Nottingham in 1847 but was declared insane in 1852, ending his career.

old age pensions: financial support for the elderly, first introduced by the Liberal government in 1908.

- Old age pensions had been debated from the early 1890s, and might have been introduced earlier but for the heavy cost of the *Anglo–Boer War, 1899–1902.*
- The Liberal scheme, associated with *Lloyd George,* was non-contributory (funded from taxation rather than insurance contributions). It was targeted at the poorest old people, and the starting age was 70.
- Contributory pensions were introduced by *Neville Chamberlain* as Minister of Health in 1925, for people aged 65 and over.

Old Poor Law: a system of assistance for the poor, created in 1597–1601 and replaced by the *New Poor Law, 1834.*

- Each parish was responsible for its own poor, and all property owners in the parish contributed money (the poor rate) for this purpose. It was administered by local officials known as overseers, who decided how the money was spent.
- Assistance was given either in the form of 'outdoor relief' (people received financial assistance to help them live in their own homes) or as 'indoor relief' (they entered a workhouse).
- The 1662 Act of Settlement said that those unable to look after themselves must receive help only in their own parish. This restricted the mobility of labour.
- By 1830, there was increasing criticism of the cost to ratepayers and of the many variations in the system over the country as a whole. This prompted the reform of 1834.

Opium Wars, 1839–42 and 1856–60: wars between Britain and China, caused by Britain's desire to gain access to Chinese markets for its trade.

- The surface issue for the wars was the export of opium from British-controlled India to China. By 1839, there were 10 million opium addicts in China, leading the Emperor to try to ban the trade. When an opium shipment was seized at Canton, Britain went to war to further its trading interests.
- The first Opium War ended in the 1842 *Treaty of Nanking*, which gave Britain Hong Kong as a base for trade in the South China Sea. The Chinese also agreed to compensate Britain for cargoes seized and opened up six ports, including Canton and Shanghai, to British trade.
- The opportunity for the second Opium War was provided by the *Arrow incident, 1856.* It ended with a march on the Chinese capital, Peking, and the burning

of the Emperor's Summer Palace. The Chinese agreed to open up the interior of their country to British trade and end restrictions on the traffic of opium.

■ *TIP* The Opium Wars are useful illustrations of *Palmerston*'s foreign policy. He was the driving force behind both wars.

Orsini affair, 1858: a political crisis caused by *Palmerston*'s attempt to change British law to prevent plots against foreign governments by refugees living in Britain.

● Felice Orsini, an Italian revolutionary, tried to assassinate the French Emperor, Napoleon III, with a bomb made in Britain. Although the Emperor survived, the French were angry with the British. In order to appease them, Palmerston decided to introduce a Conspiracy to Murder Bill, which would enable the prosecution of people who plotted against foreign governments while resident in Britain.

● This provoked an outcry in Parliament, and Palmerston (untypically) was accused of giving in to foreign pressure. His opponents united to vote against him, and he gave way to a Conservative government under *Derby*.

Osborne judgement, 1909: a legal judgement in which the *House of Lords* declared the political levy, the main method of funding for the *Labour Party*, illegal.

● When a trade union affiliated to (joined) the Labour Party, it sent a proportion of the subscription paid by its members to fund the party. This money was known as the political levy.

● W. V. Osborne, a rail union official and a Liberal supporter, objected to this and brought a court case. The House of Lords ruled that it was illegal for a political party to be funded in this way. This was a serious financial blow to the Labour Party.

● The judgement was reversed in 1913 by the Trade Union Act, passed by the Liberal government to help its Labour allies. This act allowed unions to operate the political levy, but they had to allow their members the right to 'contract out' of contributing to it if they objected.

■ *TIP* The judgement, and its reversal, are important for study of the growth of the Labour Party prior to the First World War.

Ottawa Conference, 1932: a meeting of representatives of Britain and the *Dominions*, held in Canada, to agree on trading arrangements during the *Great Depression*.

● The purpose of the conference was to enable British Commonwealth countries to help each other during the Great Depression of the early 1930s. Britain's *National Government* sent a high-profile delegation, including *Baldwin* and *Neville Chamberlain*.

● The countries agreed on a modified version of *tariff reform*, the proposal that the *British empire* should become a self-contained trading unit protected by tariffs against competition from the outside world. Instead of this, a series of bilateral agreements (involving two partners) was signed. Pairs of

Commonwealth countries agreed to give preference to each other in trade. This was because the priority for all participants was to pursue their own economic interests.

- The agreements were indicative of Britain's tendency during the 1930s to rely increasingly on empire trade when faced with difficulties in other parts of the world.

■ *TIP* The conference is important for answering exam questions on the National Government's response to the Great Depression.

Ottoman empire: see *Eastern Question.*

outdoor relief: see *Old Poor Law.*

Owen, David (1938–): see *Social Democratic Party (SDP).*

Owen, Robert (1771–1858): a factory owner and social reformer who became involved with early trade union organisation.

- Owen ran a successful textile business at New Lanark, Scotland, showing that good conditions and shorter working hours were compatible with profit making. Workers were rewarded for production, and their children received a good education, at a time when both of these were rare in the world of industry.
- He was less successful as a trade union organiser. In 1833, he founded the Grand National Consolidated Trades Union, but it survived for only 3 years. The problem was that it attempted to cover a wide variety of trades. The only unions to survive the economic depression of the late 1830s and 1840s were those that concentrated on the practical grievances of a particular trade.
- Owen was also associated with *Chartism*, but abandoned it after a section of the movement became violent.

Oxford Movement: a group within the Church of England in the 1830s and 1840s which argued that the Church was a sacred institution, created by God, and should not suffer interference from secular (non-religious) authority.

- The movement began in response to interference by Parliament under the *Whig* government of the 1830s. Its members objected to actions such as the setting up of a royal commission to investigate the revenues of the Church.
- Members were also known as 'High Church' Anglicans. They stressed the importance of tradition and ceremonial in church services. They aroused great suspicion because it was feared that they wanted to make the Church of England similar to the Catholic Church.
- Some, such as John Keble, remained Anglicans, but others (for example, John Henry Newman) eventually decided that the Church of England would never live up to their ideals, and became Roman Catholics.

Paisley, Ian (1926–): a Northern Irish Protestant clergyman and politician, founder of the Democratic Unionist Party (DUP) in 1971.

- Paisley founded the Free Presbyterian Church of Ulster in 1951. He is fiercely anti-Catholic and anti-Irish nationalist. The DUP stands for a return to a Stormont-style government of the sort which ran Northern Ireland between 1922 and 1972: Protestant-dominated, assured of its place in the UK, and free from interference by the Irish Republic.
- These views have led Paisley to be suspicious of all attempts by British governments to find a negotiated solution to the problems of Northern Ireland. He opposed the *Sunningdale Agreement, 1973*, the *Anglo–Irish Agreement, 1985*, and the *Good Friday Agreement, 1998.*

Palmerston (Henry John Temple), 3rd Viscount (1784–1865): Foreign Secretary 1830–34, 1835–41, 1846–51; Prime Minister 1855–58, 1859–65.

- Palmerston began his career as a *Liberal Tory* but joined *Grey's Whig* government in 1830.
- He was noted for his readiness to stand up for British interests, often in a forceful way, a stance which ensured him great popularity with the mid-Victorian public.
- He supported the *balance of power* created in 1815, encouraged British trade (for example, in the *Opium Wars*), opposed the slave trade and defended the rights of British citizens abroad. In 1850, in the Don Pacifico affair, he blockaded the port of Athens until the Greek government paid compensation to a British citizen from Gibraltar.
- Where feasible, he favoured the introduction of constitutional monarchy on the British model in foreign countries, believing this to be a stabilising factor. This was shown in his support for the creation of an independent Belgium in the 1830s.
- His actions were usually aggressive towards weak countries but rarely aggressive against other *Great Powers*. The exception was the *Crimean War, 1854–56* against Russia.
- In domestic affairs, Palmerston played an important role in the formation of the *Liberal Party* in 1859.

■ *TIP* Exam questions on British foreign policy in the nineteenth century will require knowledge of Palmerston's policies. Remember to state his aims if you are asked to judge his success.

Pankhurst, Emmeline (1858–1928): leader of the *suffragette* campaign for votes for women, along with her daughters, Christabel and Sylvia.

- Emmeline Pankhurst became involved in radical causes and joined the *Independent Labour Party* in the 1890s.
- As a widow, Mrs Pankhurst founded the *Women's Social and Political Union (WSPU)* in 1903. This movement had the same object as the National Union of Women's Suffrage Societies (see *Fawcett, Millicent*), but its methods were more militant. WSPU members attacked government ministers and buildings and disrupted public meetings.
- Women had not won the vote when the First World War broke out. Some historians argue that although the Pankhursts were effective self-publicists, their methods turned people against their cause.

■ *TIP* Examiners may ask you to assess the effectiveness of the Pankhursts' campaign. Did it advance or damage the cause of gaining votes for women?

Paris Peace Conference, 1919: the meeting of the victorious powers after the First World War, at which the treatment of Germany and its allies was decided and the map of Europe was redrawn.

- Britain was represented by *Lloyd George*. The other main participants were Georges Clemenceau, French Prime Minister, and Woodrow Wilson, President of the USA.
- The conference set up the *League of Nations*, which Britain joined.
- The most important treaty was that of Versailles, which stated the peace terms to be imposed on Germany. It was a harsh treaty because of the French desire for revenge and compensation for war damage, but Lloyd George acted as a moderating influence. He was concerned that a completely broken Germany might turn to *communism*.
- It was decided at the conference that the defeated powers would lose their overseas empires. Britain and France gained several territories from Germany and Turkey. These areas were known as mandates (administered by Britain and France on behalf of the League of Nations).

Paris, Treaty of, 1856: the treaty that ended the *Crimean War*, in which Britain and France had defeated Russia.

- The Black Sea was demilitarised — neither Russia nor Turkey was allowed to station a fleet there. This removed a potential naval threat to Britain in the Mediterranean.
- The powers promised to respect the independence of Turkey, and Turkey promised to improve the treatment of Christians within its empire.
- The provinces of Moldavia and Wallachia were given independence but not allowed to unite.
- It was not a permanent settlement. The Russians took advantage of the

Franco–Prussian War of 1870 to move their ships into the Black Sea. The Turkish empire was not reformed. Moldavia and Wallachia united to become Romania in 1861.

Parliament Acts, 1911 and 1949: measures that reduced the power of the *House of Lords* to obstruct bills that were started in the *House of Commons*.

- The House of Lords was dominated by Conservative peers and frequently blocked the legislation of Liberal governments. In 1909, it rejected the *People's Budget*, provoking a constitutional clash with the *Asquith* government.
- After a long struggle and two general elections (January and December 1910), the Parliament Act was passed in 1911. It reduced the maximum time between general elections from 7 years to 5. It removed the power of the Lords to block money bills (such as a budget) and allowed the Lords to delay for 2 years other bills introduced in the Commons.
- In 1949, the postwar Labour government reduced the period of delay from 2 years to 1 year.

Parliamentary reform: a gradual process by which the vote was extended to larger numbers of people and changes were made in the representation of places in Parliament.

- The electoral system at the beginning of the nineteenth century excluded large numbers of professional and business people from participation in politics. There were growing demands for this situation to be altered. The *Whig Party* was most responsive to this pressure.
- The *Industrial Revolution* had made places such as Birmingham and Leeds into important centres of population, yet they had no representation of their own in Parliament. *Rotten boroughs,* which had few or no voters, continued to return MPs to Westminster.
- The *Franchise Act, 1832* sought to rectify the most serious of these defects in the political system.

Parnell, Charles Stewart (1846–91): leader of the *Irish Nationalist Party* 1880–90.

- Parnell was an unlikely leader of the movement for Irish *Home Rule* — a Protestant landowner by background.
- He was a skilful politician who turned the Irish Nationalist Party into a disciplined force in the *House of Commons*. He cleverly exploited parliamentary rules to obstruct business and thus draw attention to the Irish cause. At the same time, he maintained links with the *Land League* and with Irish-American sources of funding. He was a central figure in the 1879 *New Departure*.
- In June 1885, he joined with the Conservatives to vote *Gladstone*'s second government out of office. In January 1886, after Gladstone decided to support Home Rule, he turned the Conservatives out. This ensured that the Liberals were committed to the Irish cause, even after the defeat of the first Home Rule Bill.
- Parnell was accused in 1887 of having written letters approving of the 1882 *Phoenix Park murders,* and was almost ruined. It was proved in 1889 that he had been framed.

- In 1890, he was cited as the guilty party in a divorce case brought by a former associate, Captain O'Shea. Parnell and Mrs O'Shea had had an affair for 10 years. This split the Irish Party, and Parnell was condemned for immorality by British Liberals and by the Catholic Church in Ireland. He died in October 1891 while trying to regain control of the party.
- *TIP* Parnell's importance lies in the fact that he came closer than any other nineteenth-century Irish leader to achieving Home Rule. You should know the reasons for his success as a leader and for his eventual fall.

paternalism: the idea that the higher social classes should care for the disadvantaged in society and that their authority should be accepted in return.

- The idea assumed a static, orderly and mainly rural society. By the early nineteenth century it was challenged by the forces of the *Industrial Revolution*.
- Paternalism partly inspired the *Ten Hours Movement* of the 1830s and 1840s and the *Young England* movement.
- The values of paternalism were emphasised by *wet Tory* critics of *Thatcherism* in the 1980s.

Peace Ballot, 1935: a questionnaire on issues of peace and disarmament, sent out to households in Britain by the *League of Nations* Union.

- The League of Nations Union was a pressure group concerned with promoting international disarmament. The questionnaire asked about a number of issues, including the question of whether economic or military methods should be used against an aggressor country.
- Over 11.5 million replies were returned. They revealed overwhelming public support for disarmament and for using economic *sanctions* against an aggressor. A smaller majority was prepared to support military measures against an aggressor.
- The ballot was taken as evidence that the British public was overwhelmingly pro-peace and pro-League of Nations.
- *TIP* The Peace Ballot is important for answering exam questions on the reasons for Britain's pursuit of a policy of *appeasement* in the 1930s.

Peel, Sir Robert (1788–1850): Chief Secretary for Ireland 1812–18; Home Secretary 1822–27, 1828–30; Prime Minister 1834–35, 1841–46. His 1834 *Tamworth Manifesto* is often taken as the foundation point of the *Conservative Party*.

- Peel had a reputation as a *Liberal Tory* in the 1820s, largely because of his reform of the criminal law as Home Secretary. He reduced the number of offences for which the death penalty could be applied. Peel founded the Metropolitan Police Force in 1829.
- An opponent of *Catholic emancipation,* he was persuaded by *Wellington* to help in passing it in 1829.
- He opposed the *Franchise Act, 1832,* but later accepted its permanence and worked to bring the Conservative Party to a realistic attitude towards the new situation.

- His government during 1841–46 introduced a number of economic reforms, including the reintroduction of *income tax* and the 1844 *Bank Charter Act*. Moves towards *free trade* led him to repeal (abolish) the *Corn Laws* in June 1846. This split the Conservative Party and put Peel out of office.
- At his death in July 1850, the result of a riding accident, Peel was celebrated as a national hero and commemorated with numerous statues and tributes.
- ■ *TIP* The key issue about Peel is whether he placed his duty to the country before the claims of his own party. You need to know why many former supporters came to see him as a traitor who betrayed Conservative principles over Catholics and corn.

Peelite: a member of the group of Conservatives who followed *Peel* over the repeal of the *Corn Laws* in 1846 and went into the political wilderness with him.

- Peelites tended to be able administrators, such as *Gladstone, Cardwell* and *Aberdeen*, who believed in an efficiently run state that did not interfere in the lives of its citizens.
- They were outnumbered by the Conservative MPs who went with *Derby* and *Disraeli*, and their numbers fell at successive general elections. They suffered the fate of a third party, trapped between the larger *Conservative* and *Whig parties*.
- Peelite ministers were important in the Aberdeen coalition of 1852–55. After it broke up, they tended to find a new political home in the *Liberal Party*.

Pentrich Rising, 1817: a failed attempt by workers in the east Midlands to start a national uprising against *Liverpool*'s government.

- The rising was an example of the desperation felt by many poor people in the period 1815–20. It focused on the Derbyshire village of Pentrich.
- It was easily suppressed by the authorities after an *agent provocateur*, W. J. Richards (known as 'Oliver the spy'), infiltrated the group. One of the leaders, Jeremiah Brandreth, was executed.
- ■ *TIP* The Pentrich Rising is important for the controversy over the handling of law and order issues by Liverpool's government. His government has traditionally been criticised for harsh measures, but you must bear in mind the lack of a regular police force and the lack of accurate knowledge about working-class movements at the time.

People's Budget, 1909: tax proposals introduced by *Lloyd George* as Chancellor of the Exchequer, which were rejected by the *House of Lords* in November 1909.

- The budget was designed to raise taxes to pay for *old age pensions* and the building of *Dreadnoughts,* both of which had proved to be expensive for the government.
- It increased existing taxes, such as income tax and death duties (tax payable by someone who inherits an estate). It also introduced a new 'supertax' on incomes over £5,000 a year and a tax on the value of land.
- The Conservatives viewed these measures as an unfair attack on wealth and the Lords rejected the budget, thus causing the crisis which led to the 1911 *Parliament Act*.

■ *TIP* Lloyd George's motives for introducing the budget are controversial. Be aware of the claim that he deliberately framed the budget in order to provide an excuse to settle the *Liberal Party*'s long-running quarrel with the Lords.

permissive legislation: laws which gave powers to local authorities to perform a particular function, but did not make it compulsory for them to act.

- Permissive legislation was common in the nineteenth century. It fitted in with ideas of *laissez-faire* (that central government should play a limited role in society). It also allowed councils to retain the favour of ratepayers (payers of local taxation), who wanted local government to be cheap.
- An example of permissive legislation is the *Artisans' Dwellings Act, 1875.*

■ *TIP* On no account should the word 'permissive' in this context be confused with the notion of a *'permissive society'*.

permissive society: a phrase associated with the Home Secretaryship of Roy *Jenkins* in the mid-1960s, meaning a more liberal (tolerant) outlook on many social issues.

- The mid-1960s witnessed a number of Acts of Parliament that extended freedom to different categories of people. The initiative did not come mainly from the Labour government of the period, but it lent its support to many of the measures.
- Examples of relevant legislation include the abolition of the death penalty for murder in 1965, and the legalisation of abortion and of homosexual acts between consenting adults in 1967. These and other measures were seen as relaxing older conventions in a number of areas.

Peterloo, 1819: the name given to the suppression of a meeting held at St Peter's Fields, Manchester, in support of parliamentary reform.

- The incident began when a peaceful crowd assembled to hear *Radical* speakers, such as 'Orator' *Hunt*, call for the extension of the vote to ordinary people and reform of the parliamentary system.
- The local authorities panicked and sent in yeomanry (mounted volunteer law enforcers) to arrest Hunt. They were unable to withdraw and so regular cavalry were sent in. Eleven people were killed and 400 injured.
- The episode was nicknamed 'Peterloo' in an ironic reference to the British victory over the French at Waterloo in 1815.
- Responsibility for the tragedy lies with the local magistrates, who over-reacted, but who lacked regular means of law enforcement such as a police force. The *Liverpool* government had doubts about their judgement but backed them up as the only available upholders of law and order.
- Following the incident, the government passed the *Six Acts* to tighten the laws on public meetings.

Phoenix Park murders, 1882: the assassination in Dublin of Lord Frederick Cavendish, newly appointed Chief Secretary for Ireland, and T. H. Burke, the senior civil servant in the British administration of Ireland.

- Cavendish had just arrived in Dublin to take up his post and was murdered, along with his chief adviser, by a group of Irish terrorists known as the Invincibles.
- The Invincibles were an extremist group, not connected with the *Irish Nationalist Party,* but the murders provoked a backlash from British public opinion against Irish nationalists of any variety. It was unfortunate that *Gladstone*, the Liberal Prime Minister, had just begun to build closer relations with the Irish leader, *Parnell,* following the *Kilmainham Treaty, 1882.* He was forced to retreat from his dealings with Parnell and revert to a tough law-and-order policy in Ireland.

Pitt, William ('the Younger') (1759–1806): Chancellor of the Exchequer 1782–83; Prime Minister 1783–1801, 1804–06.

- William Pitt 'the Younger' was the son of William Pitt 'the Elder', Earl of Chatham, who was himself Prime Minister.
- He reformed the national finances and took some steps towards *free trade* in the 1780s.
- He was Prime Minister during the French Revolutionary Wars. He aimed to defend Britain against foreign attack and its established social order against the threat of revolution.
- He put down the Irish Rising of 1798 and passed the *Act of Union, 1800*, which united Britain and Ireland under one Parliament, based in Westminster. He wanted to balance this by the introduction of *Catholic emancipation*, but failed to overcome the resistance of King George III.
- Although he never used the term 'Tory' of himself, he was an inspiration to the next generation of leaders of the party, whose careers he fostered, including *Liverpool* and *Canning.*

Plug riots, 1842: an example of the 'physical force' aspect of *Chartism,* which involved violence in parts of northern England and the Midlands.

- They were known as 'Plug' riots because protestors sabotaged industry by removing the plugs from the factory boilers.
- The year 1842 saw the most violent phase of the Chartist movement. The riots were suppressed by the authorities and sentences of imprisonment and transportation to the colonies were imposed.

plural voting: the right of certain individuals to vote in more than one constituency at general elections, which was not finally abolished until 1948.

- If people owned property in more than one constituency, this gave them the right to vote more than once.
- Oxford, Cambridge and certain other universities had their own MPs until 1948. Anyone who held the degree of Master of Arts (MA) from these universities was entitled to vote.
- These arrangements benefited the Conservatives and their allies. In the nineteenth century, for example, *Peel* was MP for Oxford University from 1817 to 1829.

pocket borough: a parliamentary constituency controlled by a powerful individual in the nineteenth century.

- Landowners not only had influence over the representation of the counties, but they also had influence in towns where they owned property. An example was Newark in Nottinghamshire, where the Duke of Newcastle ensured the election of *Gladstone* as Tory MP in 1832.
- The number of pocket boroughs was reduced by the *Franchise Act, 1832,* but they did not entirely disappear.

political levy: see *Osborne judgement.*

political unions: popular organisations created during the period 1830–32 to press for reform of Parliament and the extension of the vote.

- They helped to secure the passage of the *Franchise Act, 1832.*
- The first and most important was the Birmingham Political Union (BPU), which was formed by Thomas Attwood (1783–1856), a banker. It united middle-class and working-class supporters of reform, organising demonstrations to put pressure on the government.
- The BPU was copied in other cities. In London, a union organised by Francis Place was instrumental in preventing the anti-reform *Wellington* from forming a government in 1832. It did this by starting a 'run on the banks' — they urged small investors to withdraw their money from the banks, causing a financial panic.
- Attwood revived the BPU in 1837 in support of *Chartism.*

poll tax: see *community charge.*

postwar consensus: the idea that, between 1945 and the mid-1970s, there was broad agreement between the *Labour* and *Conservative parties* on a number of key policy areas.

- Many historians have accepted that the Second World War had a major impact on political thinking, leading both main parties to take a similar view of society. According to this view, they favoured the *mixed economy*, government action to maintain a high level of employment and a *welfare state*. This consensus broke down in the mid-1970s, when *Thatcher* took the Conservative Party in a more clear-cut, free market direction.
- Since the early 1990s, the notion of consensus has been challenged. Important continuing differences between the parties have been highlighted, for example, on how far a universal welfare system should be created. Some historians have suggested that where agreement existed, it came about because of external circumstances such as the *Cold War.*

> ■ *TIP* It is important to know why some historians, such as Paul Addison (in *The Road to 1945*, 1975), have argued that the Second World War created an unusual degree of consensus. You should also be familiar with the main arguments against the idea (for example, Kevin Jefferys, *Retreat from New Jerusalem*, 1997).

Powell, J. Enoch (1912–98): Financial Secretary to the Treasury 1957–58;

Minister of Health 1960–63; Conservative MP 1950–74; *Ulster Unionist* MP 1974–87.

- Powell was a highly intellectual backbench MP and gifted speaker, whose political influence was out of proportion to the length of his time as a minister.
- He resigned from *Macmillan*'s government in 1958 along with the Chancellor of the Exchequer, Peter Thorneycroft, and another Treasury minister, after their arguments for public-spending restrictions were rejected by their colleagues.
- He was an important influence on *Thatcherism* through his insistence on the need to control inflation through tight government spending.
- Powell was best known for his so-called 'rivers of blood' speech in April 1968, warning of the social consequences of *New Commonwealth* immigration. For this he was dismissed by *Heath* as *Conservative Party* spokesman on defence.
- He was a fervent nationalist who argued that Britain's independence was under threat from closer European integration. He left the Conservative Party in 1974 following disagreements with the leadership over Britain's entry to the *European Economic Community (EEC)* and joined the Ulster Unionists.

Pretoria Convention, 1881: a treaty between Britain and the Boer republic of the Transvaal in South Africa, which closed the *Anglo–Boer War, 1880–81*.

- Britain granted the Transvaal internal self-government, but reserved control over its foreign relations — an arrangement known as suzerainty. This was confirmed by the 1884 London Convention. It meant that the Boers did not have full independence.
- The Boers refused to accept this state of affairs in the long run. Failure to resolve the issue was a cause of the *Anglo–Boer War, 1899–1902*.

Prime Minister: the leading figure in the British government, who chairs the *Cabinet* and appoints its members.

- The first Prime Minister is generally acknowledged to have been Sir Robert Walpole (1721–42), although the title was not recognised in an Act of Parliament until 1937. The formal title of the Prime Minister is First Lord of the Treasury.
- During the nineteenth century, the growth of a *constitutional monarchy* limited the ability of the King or Queen to choose the Prime Minister. In practice, the latter was the person who could command a majority in the *House of Commons*.
- The job of Prime Minister is not formally laid down and is shaped to a large extent by the personality of the office holder.
- Since 1945, there has been recurrent controversy over the growth of prime ministerial power. Some individuals, especially *Thatcher* and *Blair*, have been accused of adopting a dominant, 'presidential' style of leadership.

Primrose League: a popular Conservative organisation, founded in 1883 by Lord *Randolph Churchill*, in memory of *Disraeli*.

- The name derives from the belief that the primrose was Disraeli's favourite flower.

- It was not officially part of the *Conservative Party*, but publicised traditional Conservative values of monarchy, religion and empire.
- It organised social events and mobilised activists, especially women, who canvassed at election time and cultivated support for the Conservatives.
- It played no part in deciding policy and never took up controversial positions within the party.
- It had 2 million members by 1910, but declined in importance after the First World War.

privatisation: the transfer of nationalised industries to the private sector, a policy associated with the Conservative governments of 1979–97.

- The Conservatives argued that the industries nationalised by the postwar Labour government were inefficiently run and that the economy would benefit from a return to free-market principles of private management and competition. They therefore sold shares in these industries to private investors.
- Examples of privatisation include the sale of British Telecom and British Airways in 1984, British Gas in 1986 and British Rail in 1994.
- Critics of the policy argued that it replaced a state monopoly with a private one. It was also argued that the money made from the sales should have been invested in long-term development rather than used to fund tax cuts.
- The Labour government elected in 1997 did not try to reverse privatisation. Indeed, it continued the policy by announcing the sale of the government interest in air-traffic control.

Profumo affair, 1963: a sex scandal that damaged the standing of *Macmillan*'s Conservative government.

- John Profumo was the Minister for War. He had an affair with a model, Christine Keeler, who was also involved with an official at the Soviet embassy, Captain Ivanov. When challenged, in March 1963, Profumo publicly denied any improper conduct. Three months later, he admitted that he had lied, and resigned from the government.
- The affair raised widespread rumours about the involvement of other well-known figures in scandalous activity. A senior judge, Lord Denning, was appointed to conduct an inquiry. Macmillan's government was attacked in the *House of Commons*, and there were suggestions (never verified) that the Soviet dimension of the affair involved a security risk.
- Although Macmillan survived — ill health, not Profumo, brought about his resignation in October 1963 — the affair damaged his reputation for competence. He seemed out of touch and the victim rather than the master of events.

proportional representation: a system of voting under which the number of votes cast for each party is proportional to the number of seats won.

- Britain uses the 'first-past-the-post' system, which has been criticised for not ensuring proportional results. It tends to exaggerate the lead of the winning party in a general election and to work against smaller parties.

- The Liberals (Liberal Democrats since 1988) have campaigned for proportional representation on grounds of fairness, but also because they have done badly since the 1920s under the current system.
- The Labour government elected in 1997 appointed a commission chaired by Lord *Jenkins*, to review the voting system, but so far has failed to act on its recommendations for general elections. A kind of proportional system was adopted in 1999 for elections to the European Parliament.

protectionism: a policy of placing taxes (duties or tariffs) on imported goods in order to protect home industries and trade.

- Protectionism was gradually abandoned between the 1820s and the 1850s, in favour of a policy of *free trade*. It was argued that protectionism favoured a few sections of the community by artificially driving up prices for British consumers.
- The most controversial example of protection was the *Corn Laws, 1815–46*, designed to maintain the profits of British farmers and landowners. Their abandonment caused a split in the ruling *Conservative Party*.
- Governments did not dare to reintroduce protection, even when farmers were suffering from foreign competition (as in the late 1870s), because the majority of people identified free trade with cheap food and rising living standards.
- In the late nineteenth century, certain sectors of the economy (for example, the metal trades) took up the cry of 'fair trade' — they wanted to see taxes placed on selected imported goods which were placing them at a commercial disadvantage.

public corporation: a body run by a board appointed by the government, but operating largely on business principles and independent of government control on a day-to-day basis.

- Governments between the wars adopted the device as a means of organising certain public services. The *Baldwin* government created two public corporations in 1926, the *British Broadcasting Corporation (BBC)* and the Central Electricity Board.
- The public corporation was the model chosen by the postwar Labour government for the running of industries and services after *nationalisation*.

Public Health Act, 1848: the first serious attempt by central government to tackle the problem of disease and poor sanitation in industrial towns and cities.

- It was prompted by recurring outbreaks of cholera, a disease associated with unclean water. *Chadwick*, author of an important 1842 report into urban sanitation problems, was the main individual pressing for change.
- It was difficult to get local authorities to do something because of the costs which ratepayers (payers of local taxation, based on property values) would have to face.
- The act gave local authorities the power to set up a Local Board of Health, supervised by a Central Board in London. The Central Board could compel an authority to set up a board if the death-rate rose above 23 per 1,000 in a year.

Local boards were able to take action to provide clean water and sewerage facilities and to dispose of 'nuisances' (rubbish) which posed a danger to public health.

- The act was the first of a number of attempts to clean up Britain's cities. The Public Health Act, 1875, which brought all of these acts together and consolidated them, is also important.

■ *TIP* The Public Health Act of 1848 was typical of Victorian social legislation, in that it was based on the 'permissive' principle (the main initiative lay with local councils). Note, however, that there was an element of compulsion where central government considered it necessary.

quango (short for 'quasi-autonomous non-government organisation'): an organisation created and funded by government, but not actually a formal part of government.

- Quangos have many different functions. Some, such as the Commission for Racial Equality, regulate a particular area of the law. Others give advice to government or look into complaints.
- Many quangos were created in the 1980s and 1990s to regulate the activities of industries and services which had undergone *privatisation*. An example is Oftel, which monitors British Telecom.
- Quangos have been criticised for being unelected and unaccountable to ordinary people.

Radical: in the nineteenth century, someone who wanted to see fundamental changes in the political system and was inspired by ideas of freedom and equality of opportunity.

● Radicals were opposed to the domination of society and government by the aristocracy, which they identified with corruption and the denial of popular rights. Among Radical causes were the extension of the vote to working people and the disestablishment of the *Anglican Church*. *Cobden* and Bright, leaders of the campaign against the *Corn Laws*, were perhaps the best-known Radicals of the nineteenth century.

● Many Radicals campaigned for single issues, which they believed to be the key to wider social progress. For example, some were members of the United Kingdom Alliance, which pressed for control of the alcoholic drink trade.

● Most Radicals found a political home in the *Liberal Party*, where their varied enthusiasms and their impatience presented the leadership with problems of party management.

▥ *TIP* Define the term 'Radical' carefully when discussing the composition and policies of the nineteenth-century Liberal Party.

Railway Act, 1844: a law to regulate the activities of the early privately owned railway companies and to provide for certain minimum standards for passengers.

● The Railway Act was the work of *Gladstone* as a member of *Peel*'s government.

● It created a Railways Board with powers of inspection and regulation.

● The most important feature of the act was the so-called parliamentary train — each company was required to put on at least one cheap train each day that stopped at every station on the line.

● The original form of the bill provided for future government intervention in the running of the railways, but this aspect was not pursued.

▥ *TIP* The Railway Act is an example of a Victorian government modifying the principle of *laissez-faire* in what it considered to be the general interest.

railway mania: a period of intense investment in the building of railways.

● There were two main phases of railway mania, 1836–38 and 1844–48. In the second phase, money spent on railway development accounted for half of the private investment in Britain. More than 2,000 miles of track were opened in this period.

- The mania generated an enormous volume of employment and stimulated other industries, especially coal, iron and engineering.
- Many of the smaller companies created earlier were amalgamated into larger concerns.
- Fortunes were made and lost. The best-known example is George Hudson (1800–71), known as the 'railway king' until his dishonest business methods led to his downfall in 1849.

real wages: the value of money wages when set against changes in prices (an individual's purchasing power).

- Real wages are a better guide than money wages for historians investigating changes in people's living standards.
- For those who kept their jobs, real wages remained consistently higher during the *Great Depression* than they had been before the First World War. This was because prices fell faster than wages. It helps to explain why some historians do not present the 1920s and 1930s as a time of unrelieved economic distress.

Rebecca riots, 1842–43: a series of protests in west Wales against high turnpike tolls and tithes paid to the *Anglican Church*.

- Turnpikes were toll gates set up to collect money from travellers for the upkeep of roads. Tithes were a tax of one-tenth of agricultural produce, paid to the established Church in England and Wales.
- These events were known as 'Rebecca riots' because the protestors disguised themselves as women. They took their name from a verse in the Book of Genesis, 'the seed of Rebecca shall possess the gates of her enemies'.

referendum: a vote taken on a single issue, usually one with far-reaching constitutional or economic significance.

- The only UK-wide referendum to date was held in 1975, on the question of whether Britain should stay in the *European Economic Community (EEC)*. This is usually interpreted as having been a device of the Labour Prime Minister, *Wilson*, to paper over the divisions within his own party on Europe.
- The *Callaghan* government held referendums in Wales and Scotland in 1979 on whether the inhabitants wanted to see *devolution* for these parts of the UK. Support did not meet the specified threshold of 40% of the total population.
- In the 1997 general election, the Referendum Party, led by the millionaire businessman Sir James Goldsmith, called for a British referendum on the issue of participation in the further development of the European Union.
- The *Blair* government held referendums in 1997 on Welsh and Scottish devolution, and this time the proposals were approved.
- A referendum has been suggested as a way of resolving the long-running debate over whether Britain should join a single European currency.

Reform Acts: see *Franchise Acts, 1832, 1867, 1884, 1918.*

Relugas Compact, 1905: an informal agreement between *Asquith*, Sir Edward Grey and *Haldane*, to undermine the authority of Liberal Party leader, *Campbell-Bannerman*.

- Asquith, Grey and Haldane were leading *Liberal imperialist* politicians who wanted to sideline Campbell-Bannerman. They agreed not to join a Liberal government unless he became a figurehead prime minister in the House of Lords.
- The compact was agreed at Relugas, Grey's fishing lodge in Scotland.
- In the event, the three men accepted office under Campbell-Bannerman without conditions when he formed a government 3 months later.
- ■ *TIP* Although the compact was a non-starter, its existence is an example of the divisions in the Liberal Party in the period 1894–1905.

Rhodes, Cecil (1853–1902): an imperial adventurer who founded *Rhodesia* as a result of his business exploits in southern Africa.

- The son of a clergyman, Rhodes went out to Africa and made a fortune in diamond mining. He aimed to increase his personal wealth and extend the *British empire* in southern Africa. His long-term ambition was to oversee the conquest of an expanse of territory 'from the Cape to Cairo' (from the southern tip of Africa to Egypt).
- His ambitions led him into conflict with the native peoples of the region and with the Boers, who ran the Transvaal. His British South Africa Company controlled the area that became known as Rhodesia.
- Rhodes was Prime Minister of Cape Colony from 1890 to 1896. He was forced to resign because of his involvement in the *Jameson raid*.

Rhodesia (Zimbabwe since 1980): African territory settled by the British South Africa Company under *Rhodes* in the 1890s.

- Rhodesia joined with nearby Nyasaland to form the Central African Federation from 1953 to 1964. This broke up because of black African opposition to white dominance. Northern Rhodesia became independent as Zambia.
- Southern Rhodesia continued under white minority rule. Britain refused to grant it independence on these terms, partly because it would offend African and Asian opinion in the Commonwealth. The white government of Ian Smith made a 'unilateral declaration of independence' in November 1965 and resisted British pressure for a compromise with its black population.
- Smith finally reached an agreement with moderate black leaders in 1978. This did not satisfy the 'Patriotic Front' of Joshua Nkomo and Robert Mugabe, who waged a guerrilla war from bases in neighbouring countries. In 1979, Britain agreed to elections in which the Patriotic Front could take part. This brought about the creation of an independent Zimbabwe under black majority rule.
- ■ *TIP* The long-running Rhodesian problem was a major embarrassment for Britain for 15 years. At a time when *decolonisation* was proceeding rapidly, Britain was unable to shed its responsibilities in Rhodesia on terms acceptable to the Commonwealth.

Rosebery (Archibald Philip Primrose), 5th Earl of (1847–1929): Foreign Secretary 1886, 1892–94; Prime Minister 1894–95; leader of the *Liberal Party* 1894–96.

- Rosebery was a *Liberal imperialist* who tried to lead the Liberal Party away from its commitment under *Gladstone* to 'little England' issues such as *Home Rule* for Ireland. He wanted a Liberal Party that took a positive view of the empire, and linked this with support for reform. He was the first chairman of the London County Council in 1889.
- In foreign affairs, he aimed for continuity of policy with the Conservatives on the main issues.
- He was ineffectual as Prime Minister. *Nonconformists* and serious reformers in the party regarded him as an unsuitable choice because of his relaxed aristocratic style and his love of horse-racing.
- Rosebery's government was dominated by the feud waged by the Chancellor of the Exchequer, Sir William Harcourt, against his authority. He resigned on a minor issue in June 1895. He then led the party to a crushing defeat in the ensuing general election.
- *TIP* Rosebery is important for a study of the decline of the Liberal Party in the 1890s and early 1900s.

Rothermere (Harold Harmsworth), 1st Viscount (1868–1940): younger brother of *Northcliffe*, whom he succeeded as head of Associated Newspapers, the group that controlled the **Daily Mail** and **Daily Mirror**.

- Rothermere served as Air Minister from 1917 to 1918 under *Lloyd George*.
- He collaborated with Beaverbrook, owner of the **Daily Express**, in the 1929–31 campaign to get the *Conservative Party* to adopt a policy of 'empire free trade', an updated version of *tariff reform*. They created the United Empire Party and ran candidates against official Conservative candidates at by-elections.
- Rothermere briefly supported *Mosley*'s British Union of Fascists because of its anti-communism, but abandoned it after violence at the 1934 Olympia meeting.

rotten borough: a parliamentary constituency which continued to return MPs to Westminster although it no longer had many voters. Many were controlled by one powerful patron.

- Rotten boroughs were one of the worst abuses of the pre-1832 electoral system. They were an extreme demonstration of the way in which the old system failed to relate population movements to parliamentary representation. Parliamentary reformers wanted to end the separate representation of these boroughs.
- Examples of rotten boroughs include Old Sarum in Wiltshire, an earthwork, and Dunwich, on the Suffolk coast, which had largely disappeared into the sea by the nineteenth century.
- The *Franchise Act, 1832* abolished most rotten boroughs.

Russell, Lord John (1st Earl Russell) (1792–1878): Paymaster General 1830–34; Home Secretary 1835–39; Secretary for War and the Colonies 1839–41; Prime Minister 1846–52, 1865–66; Foreign Secretary 1852–53, 1859–65;

Lord President of the Council 1854–55; Secretary for the Colonies 1855.

- Russell was a leading *Whig* who played a major role in the repeal of the *Test and Corporation Acts* in 1828 and the passage of the *Franchise Act, 1832.*
- As Prime Minister in 1846–52, he passed useful legislation including the *Public Health Act, 1848.*
- He was opposed to *Chartism.*
- As Prime Minister in 1865–66, he tried and failed to pass a bill extending the vote beyond the 1832 limits.
- Russell tended to be overshadowed by stronger colleagues and rivals, especially *Palmerston,* with whom he co-operated in the formation of the *Liberal Party* at the Willis's Rooms meeting, 1859.

sale of honours: the practice of awarding titles of honour in return for donations, associated with the *Lloyd George coalition* in the early 1920s.

- Political parties had given peerages and other honours to important donors for many years, but under Lloyd George there was a widespread feeling that the practice was being abused.
- One award in particular, the proposal to make a South African financier, Sir J. B. Robinson, a member of the *House of Lords*, was the subject of a parliamentary debate in 1922.
- The scandal contributed to the growing unpopularity of Lloyd George and to his downfall following the *Carlton Club revolt, 1922.*

Salisbury (Robert Gascoyne Cecil), 3rd Marquess of (1830–1903): Secretary for India 1866–67, 1874–78; Foreign Secretary 1878–80, 1885–86, 1887–92, 1895–1900; Prime Minister 1885–86, 1886–92, 1895–1902; leader of the *Conservative Party* 1881–1902 (from 1881 to 1885, jointly with Sir Stafford Northcote).

- Salisbury was known as Viscount Cranborne until 1868, when he succeeded to the title of Lord Salisbury.
- He was noted as a young man for his hard-line Conservative views; he resigned in protest at the *Franchise Act, 1867,* which he saw as too democratic.
- As Foreign Secretary he represented Britain at the *Berlin Congress* in 1878.
- He became more flexible in his defence of Conservative principles with the passage of time, working effectively with the *Liberal Unionists* after the 1886 *Home Rule* crisis split the *Liberal Party.*
- Salisbury did much to improve the organisation of the Conservative Party, focusing on the cultivation of suburban middle-class 'villa Toryism'.
- He was an effective party leader, retaining office in the general election of 1885 and securing outright victory in 1886, 1895 and 1900.
- His main interest was in foreign affairs, where he promoted British interests by remaining semi-detached from European commitments. His support for imperial expansion during the *Scramble for Africa* assisted the electoral success of the Conservative Party.

▓ *TIP* It is important to know the reasons for the Conservative Party's domination of the political scene under Salisbury.

sanctions: penalties (usually economic) imposed on one country by others, in order to influence its conduct.

- The *League of Nations* had the authority to get its members to impose economic sanctions on a country that had committed an act of aggression. This meant that they would agree to suspend their trade with that country. Sanctions were imposed on Italy in the *Abyssinian War*, but their effectiveness was limited by the omission of oil. They failed to prevent Italy from conquering Abyssinia.
- The international community imposed sanctions on *Rhodesia* after its Unilateral Declaration of Independence (UDI) in 1965, but it was able to get around the restrictions with the help of its neighbour, South Africa. The guerrilla war waged by black nationalist forces was more important in the defeat of the Rhodesian regime.

school board: see *Education Act, 1870.*

Scottish National Party (SNP): a political party formed in 1934 to campaign for Scotland's independence.

- The SNP was not a significant force until the early 1970s. It won 11 seats in the October 1974 general election, pressing for *devolution.*
- The discovery of North Sea oil, which was exploited from 1975, helped the nationalist cause. They argued that it was Scotland's oil and could be the basis of a thriving economy, enabling independence within the *European Economic Community.*
- The Conservative governments of 1979–97 stimulated Scottish support for devolution by policies that seemed to be imposed without consultation from London, such as the piloting of the *community charge* before its introduction in England.
- The SNP welcomed the creation of the Scottish Parliament by the Labour government elected in 1997, viewing it as a step towards greater independence.

Scramble for Africa: the expansion of European control of Africa, which was at its most intense between about 1880 and 1900.

- Britain was the main gainer of the 'scramble', becoming increasingly involved after occupying Egypt in 1882.
- Historians have disagreed about the reasons for the scramble. Some have stressed the importance of trade and investment. Others have explained it with reference to rivalry among the *Great Powers*, or to the need to protect missionary work and to abolish the slave trade.
- One of the most influential explanations, put forward by R. Robinson and J. Gallagher in ***Africa and the Victorians*** (1961), stressed the importance of strategic calculations surrounding the security of sea routes to India.

  ▉ *TIP* Questions on the Scramble for Africa require knowledge of the factors promoting British involvement. Avoid broad generalisations and look instead at why Britain was interested in particular parts of Africa.

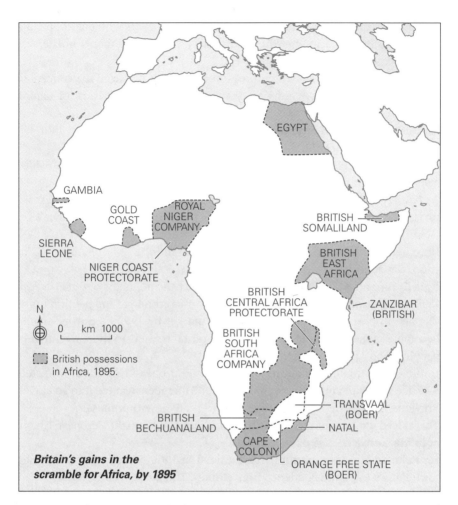

GAMBIA

GOLD
COAST

ROYAL
NIGER
COMPANY

EGYPT

SIERRA
LEONE

NIGER COAST
PROTECTORATE

BRITISH
SOMALILAND

BRITISH
EAST
AFRICA

BRITISH
CENTRAL AFRICA
PROTECTORATE

ZANZIBAR
(BRITISH)

N

0   km 1000

British possessions
in Africa, 1895.

BRITISH
SOUTH
AFRICA
COMPANY

BRITISH
BECHUANALAND

TRANSVAAL
(BOER)

NATAL

CAPE
COLONY

*Britain's gains in the
scramble for Africa, by 1895*

ORANGE FREE STATE
(BOER)

SDF: see *Social Democratic Federation.*

SDLP: see *Social Democratic and Labour Party.*

SDP: see *Social Democratic Party.*

secret ballot, 1872: a reform introduced by the first *Gladstone* government, allowing voters to cast their vote at general elections by making a cross on a ballot paper in private.

● *Radicals* had demanded the secret ballot throughout the nineteenth century in order to protect voters from intimidation by their employers or landlords. Until 1872, voting was done in public.

● This did not end electoral corruption, which had to be tackled by the *Corrupt and Illegal Practices Act, 1883.*

Shaftesbury, Earl of: see *evangelicalism.*

Sheffield outrages, 1866: the use of violence by trade unionists in Sheffield, south Yorkshire, against individual workers whose refusal to join a union threatened the wage levels of the rest.

- Explosives were used in an attempt to intimidate workers who did not belong to a union involved in the Sheffield cutlery trade. One man's house was blown up.
- Although this was an isolated outbreak of violence, it damaged the concept of trade unionism in the eyes of property owners and set back the cause of gaining legal recognition for unions.

Sidmouth, Viscount (Henry Addington) (1757–1844): Prime Minister 1801–04; Home Secretary 1812–22.

- As Prime Minister, Addington negotiated the Treaty of Amiens, which provided a short break in the conflict with revolutionary France.
- As *Liverpool*'s Home Secretary, he was associated with the so-called 'repressive' phase of the ministry prior to 1822. He was the author of the *Six Acts, 1819*.
- He served in the *Cabinet* without office from 1822 to 1824.
- In retirement, he opposed *Catholic emancipation* and the *Franchise Act, 1832*.

Simon, Sir John: see *Liberal National*.

Single European Act, 1985–86: an agreement by the members of the *European Economic Community (EEC)* to move towards closer economic and political unity.

- The act proposed the creation of a single market by 1992 — Europe would become a single economic unit, with no internal barriers to the movement of people, goods and investment.
- It introduced qualified majority voting in the European Council of Ministers — a decision could be taken even if not all the members wanted it to go ahead. Previously, states had had the right to veto (vote down) proposals.
- This moved the Community towards its transformation into the European Union.

single market: see *Single European Act*.

Sinn Fein: an Irish republican party, founded in 1906, which has campaigned for Ireland's total independence from Britain. The name means 'ourselves'.

- Originally, Sinn Fein supported a dual nationality solution for Ireland's relationship with Britain. The model was the monarchy of Austria–Hungary. It adopted a republican solution in 1917.
- Sinn Fein was founded by Arthur Griffith who, with Michael Collins, negotiated the *Anglo–Irish Treaty, 1921*. Sinn Fein split over the treaty, with a section of the party objecting to the fact that the British monarch remained head of state.
- It is associated with the *IRA*; members of the Unionist community regard it as the political wing of a terror campaign to remove Northern Ireland from the UK.
- Sinn Fein supported the *Good Friday Agreement, 1998* and participated in the Northern Ireland assembly.

Six Acts, 1819 (also called the 'Gag Acts'): measures introduced by the *Liverpool* government to restrict protests by *Radicals* who were demanding greater political rights and parliamentary reform.

- The Six Acts were introduced by the Home Secretary, Viscount *Sidmouth*, after *Peterloo, 1819*.

- They placed restrictions on public meetings, made it harder for Radicals to publish literature attacking the government, and gave magistrates powers to search for concealed weapons.
- The acts were viewed as unacceptably repressive by Radicals at the time, but were relatively mild by comparison with measures introduced in several European countries. Several aspects of the acts were temporary measures, designed to deal with an immediately threatening situation, and were not renewed in calmer times.

slump: see *Great Depression.*

Snowden, Philip (1864–1937): a founder of the *Independent Labour Party* in 1893; Chancellor of the Exchequer 1924, 1929–31; Lord Privy Seal 1931–32.

- Regarded as the *Labour Party*'s financial expert, Snowden took a strictly conventional view of economic management. He believed that a Labour government must balance the budget and maintain confidence in the value of the pound. Progress towards socialism must be gradual and non-revolutionary.
- He supported *MacDonald* in his decision to form the *National Government* in August 1931. He later resigned from the government in protest at its decision to abandon *free trade.*

SNP: see *Scottish National Party.*

Social Darwinism: the belief that the course of human history is determined by a struggle between strong and weak races.

- Social Darwinism was a perversion of the teaching of Charles Darwin (1809–82) about the 'survival of the fittest' in the animal world. It became popular on the right of British politics in the 1890s and early 1900s.
- Supporters of the theory applied it to the rise of Anglo–German rivalry prior to the First World War. It influenced sections of the press and some Conservative politicians. It helped to create the kind of atmosphere where war was a possibility, although it is not easy to detect its specific influence on the government that took the decision for war in 1914.

Social Democratic and Labour Party (SDLP): a leading Catholic nationalist party in Northern Ireland, founded in 1970, which favours the unification of Ireland by peaceful means.

- The SDLP began as the champion of Catholic civil rights during the early stages of the *Troubles.*
- It was founded by Gerry Fitt and has been led since 1979 by John Hume.
- It played an important part in the *Sunningdale Agreement, 1973*, the *Anglo–Irish Agreement, 1985* and the *Good Friday Agreement, 1998.*
- The party was a rival of *Sinn Fein* for the support of the Catholic population of Northern Ireland.

Social Democratic Federation (SDF): a socialist grouping, formed in 1884 by Henry Hyndman and others, which favoured Marxist ideas of class struggle.

- The SDF organised a number of working-class protests in the 1880s, but never gained mass support for its ideas of revolution.

- It helped to form the Labour Representation Committee (later to become the *Labour Party*) in 1900, but broke its connections with it soon afterwards. Most SDF members moved to the Communist Party of Great Britain after the First World War.

Social Democratic Party (SDP): a centre party, created in 1981 by a group of former Labour ministers, which eventually amalgamated with the *Liberal Party.*

- The SDP was started by the so-called 'Gang of Four', a group of senior Labour figures who had become frustrated by the leftward drift of the party. They were Roy *Jenkins,* David Owen (former Foreign Secretary), Shirley Williams (former Education Secretary) and Bill Rodgers (former Transport Secretary).
- The SDP stood for the retention of Britain's nuclear weapons, staying in the *EEC* and the *mixed economy* — all policies that the *Labour Party* was abandoning.
- It formed an electoral alliance with the Liberal Party in 1983. SDP supporters found common ground with the Liberals at local level, and by 1988 a merger of the two parties had become logical. Owen could not accept this and led a minority, who continued independently until 1990. The majority merged with the Liberals to form the Liberal Democrat Party.
- *TIP* The formation of the SDP helped to split the opposition to the Conservatives in the 1980s and was a factor in the success of Margaret *Thatcher.*

socialism: the belief that a fairer, more equal society can be created through state ownership of key sections of the economy.

- *Clause Four* of the *Labour Party*'s Constitution, adopted in 1918, contains the classic definition of socialism as the common (state) ownership of the means of production, distribution and exchange.
- After the *nationalisation* measures of the *Attlee* government in the late 1940s, some Labour thinkers began to redefine socialism in terms of equality and social justice, rather than further state ownership of industry. This was advanced by Anthony Crosland, an associate of *Gaitskell,* in **The Future of Socialism**, published in 1956.
- *TIP* Be sure to define socialism carefully in essay answers on the Labour Party. Do not confuse it with *communism.*

Spa Fields Riots, 1816: two demonstrations against the *Liverpool* government, organised by members of a revolutionary group known as the Spenceans.

- The Spenceans included Arthur Thistlewood, later responsible for the *Cato Street conspiracy, 1820.*
- The protest meetings were peaceful until a breakaway group attacked a gunsmith's shop and tried to take over the Tower of London.
- The incident illustrated the weakness of the revolutionary threat to the government. Prominent *Radicals* avoided the meetings and 'Orator' *Hunt,* who addressed the first gathering, made a point of condemning violence.

Special Areas Act, 1934: an attempt by the *National Government* to direct investment into areas of particularly high unemployment during the *Great Depression.*

- The areas selected for government action were South Wales, northeast England, West Cumberland and Clydeside. All were associated with the old, declining *staple industries* of coal or shipbuilding.
- The level of funding allocated to the scheme was not high enough to have more than a limited effect on unemployment. The rearmament programme, which was begun the following year, was more significant for the creation of jobs.

Speenhamland system: a method of assisting poor labourers at times of high food prices, first introduced in 1795 and copied in parts of southern and central England.

- The system takes its name from the village of Speenhamland in Berkshire, where magistrates responsible for the poor met to decide how to prevent starvation at a time of rapid price rises. They devised a system of allowances, where the amount given depended on bread prices and the size of the needy person's family.
- Critics of the *Old Poor Law* were particularly opposed to Speenhamland, arguing that it encouraged the poor to have large families and discouraged them from working hard. It was one of the reasons for the introduction of the *New Poor Law, 1834*.

splendid isolation: a popular description of British foreign policy in the late nineteenth century, particularly associated with *Salisbury*, suggesting a studied detachment from European affairs.

- Historians now qualify the use of this phrase. It is true that Britain's world-wide empire and lack of a large army dictated limited involvement in European alliances. Salisbury was anxious to avoid open-ended commitments, which might have involved Britain in war.
- Nonetheless, he was prepared to enter into arrangements with other powers, where Britain's interests would be furthered and where the commitments were clearly defined. The *Mediterranean Agreements, 1887* are an example of this approach.

Stanley: see *Derby, 14th Earl of*.

staple industries: the older, heavy industries which were the basis of Britain's *Industrial Revolution*: coal, textiles, iron and steel, and shipbuilding. They depended on exporting their products.

- By 1914, these industries were in a vulnerable economic position, as rival countries, which industrialised later, enjoyed the benefits of more modern technology and methods. Foreign countries such as Germany and the USA protected their industries with import duties, while Britain clung to a policy of *free trade* until the early 1930s.
- The First World War made the position of Britain's staple industries worse, by disrupting patterns of trade. This meant that overseas customers reduced their imports from Britain. In the Far East, Japan moved into markets which had once been open to British goods.

- In 1925, the British government returned to the *gold standard* at the pre-war rate of exchange, which made British exports too expensive. As a result, the staple industries were hard hit by the *Great Depression* of the late 1920s and early 1930s.
- The decline of the staple industries led to mass unemployment in certain areas of the country — northern England, South Wales and southwest Scotland.

Stephenson, George (1781–1848) and Robert (1803–59): father and son engineers who promoted the growth of the steam railway.

- George Stephenson is well known for the early steam engine, the 'Rocket', and for the building of the Stockton to Darlington Railway (1825) in northeast England. The latter was the first commercially successful railway and persuaded many people to invest in the growth of railways.
- Robert worked with his father on railway projects. He was personally responsible for the Tyne Bridge at Newcastle (1849) and the Menai Straits Bridge to Anglesey in North Wales (1850).

sterling area: the group of empire/Commonwealth countries, linked to Britain after the Second World War, who agreed to have the pound sterling as their reserve currency.

- Britain believed that as the *British empire* was transformed into a Commonwealth of self-governing states, the sterling area would enable it to retain influence and strength in the world. It meant that empire countries built up large sterling balances and Britain acted as banker to those countries.
- By the late 1950s, there were concerns about the economic value of the sterling area. Britain's declining earnings from its exports called into question its ability to supply funds to the sterling area.

stop–go policies: the name given to rapid changes in government economic policy between the 1950s and the 1970s, a period when Britain's relative trade position was in decline.

- During the 'go' phase, large quantities of imports entered the country, leading to high consumer spending and wage demands. Governments feared the return of *inflation* and imposed restrictions in the 'stop' phase, such as higher taxes and higher interest rates, which made borrowing more expensive.
- These restrictions would be relaxed in the run-up to a general election, in order to win popularity. An example of this was the Conservative policy of a 'dash for growth' in 1963–64.
- The 'stop–go' cycle was criticised by many economists for the way in which it made it hard for industry to plan ahead. It was accused of preventing the sustained, steady growth of the economy.

Stormont: see *direct rule*.

Strange Death of Liberal England, The: the title of a widely read book, first published in 1935, by the journalist and popular historian George Dangerfield. He argued that in the years 1910–14, the *Liberal Party* was fatally damaged by a series of crises.

- Liberal ideology was based on respect for constitutional practice and reason. It was therefore ill-suited to the fourfold challenge of *House of Lords* opposition to the *Parliament Act,* militant trade unionism, the *suffragettes* and the *Ulster Crisis, 1912–14.*
- Not all historians accept the Dangerfield theory. Some, such as Peter Clarke, author of **Lancashire and the New Liberalism** (1971), argue that the pre-war Liberal government was winning working-class support with social reform policies. In **The Downfall of the Liberal Party** (1966), Trevor Wilson located the real crisis of the party in the First World War.

▨ TIP It is worth familiarising yourself with the arguments for and against the view that the Liberal Party was in terminal decline by 1914. Be able to quote a few historians on both sides of the argument.

Suez Canal: an international waterway running through Egypt, linking the Mediterranean and the Red Sea and providing a short cut for British ships travelling to India and the Far East.

- The canal was dug by a French engineer, Ferdinand de Lesseps, and was opened in 1869.
- *Disraeli* bought shares for Britain in 1875 and, until 1956, the canal was controlled by an Anglo–French company.
- Britain occupied Egypt in 1882, after a nationalist revolt threatened the security of the canal. British troops remained in the Suez Canal Zone until withdrawn, following negotiations with the Egyptian government, in 1954.

Suez Crisis, 1956: an international crisis caused by Egyptian President Nasser's decision to nationalise the *Suez Canal* (bring it under Egyptian government control).

- Nasser was an Egyptian nationalist who wanted to reduce Western influence in his country. After Britain and the USA withdrew their financial support for the building of the Aswan Dam, he decided to seize the Suez Canal and use its revenues to fund the dam project.
- After several months of attempted American mediation, Britain and France invaded Egypt in November 1956 to recover the canal by force. They did this following a secret agreement with Israel, which was an enemy of Egypt.
- The invasion outraged world opinion and the USA brought pressure to bear on Britain, compelling a withdrawal from Egypt.
- The failure caused the downfall of Prime Minister *Eden,* who had ordered the attack. It damaged Britain's standing in the Middle East and demonstrated the impossibility of taking isolated military action against the wishes of the USA.

▨ TIP According to some historians, the crisis accelerated Britain's withdrawal from imperial commitments. It is an important episode for the study of *decolonisation.*

suffragette: a member of the *Women's Social and Political Union (WSPU),* founded in 1903 by Emmeline *Pankhurst* and her daughters, which used militant means to draw attention to the demand for votes for women.

● The name 'suffragette' was coined by the ***Daily Mail*** in 1906. It was a variation of the term 'suffragist' and was intended to belittle the women campaigners. Nonetheless, the name stuck and lost its insulting connotations.

Sunningdale Agreement, 1973: an attempt by the *Heath* government to end political violence in Northern Ireland by creating a power-sharing executive — a government containing representatives of both the *Ulster Unionist* and the nationalist communities.

● The agreement was supported by moderate Unionists and nationalists of the *Social Democratic and Labour Party (SDLP)*. It was also supported by the government of the Irish Republic, which agreed to meet representatives of Northern Ireland in a Council of Ireland.

● It was opposed by hard-line Unionists such as *Paisley*, leader of the Democratic Unionist Party (DUP). They formed part of the Ulster Workers' Council, which brought an end to the power-sharing executive by organising a general strike in May 1974.

suzerainty: an arrangement whereby a country has freedom to control its own internal affairs but its foreign policy is managed by another country.

● The classic example in this period is the situation of the Boers after the *Pretoria Convention, 1881*. It was a cause of the resentment which produced the second *Anglo–Boer War* of 1899–1902.

syndicalism: a revolutionary movement among trade unions before the First World War, whose object was to bring about a general strike and to undermine the capitalist system.

● The idea came from France, where it was developed by the socialist thinker Georges Sorel. In Britain, it was supported by Tom Mann, an organiser of the *London Dock Strike, 1889*.

● Syndicalists rejected the idea of working through Parliament for improved working-class conditions, and called instead for direct strike action to achieve their aims.

● The movement was blamed for the high level of strike activity in the period 1910–14, but it seems that its influence has been exaggerated. Most trade unionists preferred to use legal methods and were more concerned with specific improvements in wages and conditions than with broader political objectives.

▓ *TIP* You will need to know about syndicalism for exam questions on the rise of Labour or the decline of the Liberals before 1914.

Taff Vale Case, 1900–01: a court case in which the *House of Lords* ruled that a trade union was liable for the damages suffered by a railway company during strike action.

- The Taff Vale Railway Company in South Wales sued the Amalgamated Society of Railway Servants for the losses incurred during a strike. The case went to the House of Lords, which awarded the company £23,000 in damages, plus costs.
- This effectively crippled the strike as a weapon in industrial disputes. It played a part in losing the Conservatives the working-class vote in the 1906 general election, since they failed to pass a law to reverse the judgement.
- *MacDonald*, the secretary of the recently founded Labour Representation Committee, used the case as an argument to persuade trade unions to support the LRC.
- The Liberal government passed the 1906 Trades Disputes Act to satisfy its Labour allies. This gave the unions legal immunity against civil actions of the Taff Vale kind.
- **TIP** Taff Vale is an important issue in the rise of Labour before 1914. It is worth knowing what was at issue in the case.

Tamworth Manifesto, 1834: a statement of *Conservative Party* attitudes by Sir Robert *Peel*. Although formally addressed to his constituency of Tamworth in Staffordshire, it was really aimed at a national audience.

- The Tamworth Manifesto is often taken as the point when the older *Tory Party* was changed into the Conservative Party.
- It made clear the party's acceptance of changes following the *Franchise Act, 1832*. The party still stood for the traditional establishment in both Church and state, but it would be prepared to reform 'proven abuses' and to redress (put right) 'real grievances'. It would not support change for its own sake.
- This manifesto is often seen as a bid to broaden support for the party, beyond its historic rural, landowning base, to include the rising middle classes.
- **TIP** Familiarity with the Tamworth Manifesto is important for exam questions on Peel and his contribution to the making of the Conservative Party.

tariff reform (also called 'imperial preference'): a policy proposed by *Joseph*

t

Chamberlain in 1903, for Britain and its empire to form a single economic bloc, protected against the outside world.

- Britain and the empire countries would impose high tariffs (taxes) on goods imported from non-empire countries. When trading with each other, they would impose lower rates of tax.
- The policy was a challenge to *free trade* economics and fractured the unity of the *Conservative Party*.
- Supporters (known as 'wholehoggers') argued that tariff reform would cement the unity of the empire, while also protecting British industry and jobs. Opponents (*'free fooders'*) said that it would raise the cost of imported food. Moderates, led by the Prime Minister, *Balfour*, favoured retaliatory tariffs against specified imports rather than an all-embracing policy of imperial preference.
- Defence of free trade helped to unite the *Liberal Party* and make possible its victory in the 1906 general election.
- A modified version of the policy was introduced in 1932 at the *Ottawa Conference*, in an attempt to counter the world depression.

Temperance Movement: a nineteenth-century campaign to limit the sale of alcoholic drink.

- Several influential pressure groups, such as the United Kingdom Alliance (founded 1853), believed that drink was a major cause of working-class poverty and other social problems. These people viewed their campaign as a moral crusade.
- They tended to be *Radicals* and *nonconformists* who found their political home in the *Liberal Party*, but it never went far enough to satisfy their demands. *Gladstone* believed that his moderate Licensing Act of 1872 helped to lose him the 1874 general election. It failed to please the temperance lobby, but at the same time led to allegations that the Liberals were depriving working people of their freedom to drink.
- Hard-liners wanted the introduction of the 'local veto', giving ratepayers in a particular area the option to vote on whether to prohibit the sale of drink.
- *TIP* The Temperance Movement is important for the study of Gladstone's Liberal Party. It illustrates the difficulties he had in maintaining the unity of a party that contained so many different pressure groups.

tenant right: the demand for farmers who rented land in Ireland to be given greater security against eviction and excessively high rents.

- The vulnerability of tenant farmers to eviction from their farms was one of the key components of the *Irish Question* in the nineteenth century.
- British governments, which were dominated by the landowning classes, were reluctant to interfere in property rights to help the tenants. *Palmerston* famously said that 'tenant's right is landlord's wrong'.
- Some steps to ease the situation were taken by *Gladstone* with his *Irish Land Acts, 1870 and 1881*.

Ten Hours Movement: a protest movement in the 1830s and 1840s that aimed to limit hours of work in textile factories.

- Supporters of the movement aimed to build on earlier *Factory Acts* aimed at protecting workers, especially women and children, from exploitation by mill owners.
- The Ten Hours Movement united Tories such as *Oastler* and people involved in working-class protests such as *Chartism*. They were motivated by a shared disapproval of the social consequences of the *Industrial Revolution*. They felt that manufacturers were pursuing profit at the expense of workers' health and well-being.
- Women and young people received a 10-hour working day by law in 1847, while adult male textile workers had to wait until 1853.

Ten Year Rule: a government ruling on defence spending, first introduced in 1919, which made the assumption that Britain would not be involved in a major war in the next 10 years.

- The rule fitted with the desire of both politicians and the public in the 1920s to avoid the build-up of large arms stocks. The costs of defence were a factor in the policy of *appeasement* pursued in this period.
- The rule was abandoned in 1932, after evidence of Japanese aggression in China raised the issue of the *British empire*'s vulnerability in the Far East. This signalled a cautious move towards rearmament.

Test and Corporation Acts repeal, 1828: the abolition of two seventeenth-century measures to exclude non-members of the *Anglican Church* from public office. They were repealed (cancelled) by Lord John *Russell* in 1828.

- The repeal was largely symbolic since Protestant *nonconformists* had found ways of getting around the acts for many years.
- The importance of the repeal lay in the way it contributed to divisions in the governing *Tory Party*. Although not as controversial as *Catholic emancipation*, it aroused the anger of right-wing Tories who regarded the Church of England as the cornerstone of the constitution.

TIP The repeal usefully illustrates the *Whig* commitment to religious toleration for Protestant nonconformists.

Thatcher, Margaret (1925–): Education Secretary 1970–74; leader of the *Conservative Party* 1975–90; Prime Minister 1979–90.

- Thatcher became Conservative leader by challenging *Heath* after he lost the two general elections of 1974.
- She described herself as a 'conviction politician' who set out to break the *postwar consensus* and move the Conservative Party in a more clearly free market direction.
- She abandoned the paternalistic *wet Tory* tradition associated with several of her recent predecessors.
- She won three general elections, in 1979, 1983 and 1987.
- Her style of leadership was combative, arousing extremes of admiration and

dislike. This was demonstrated in the *Falklands War, 1982* and in her government's defeat of the miners' strike of 1984–85.

- After 1987, she seemed increasingly politically insensitive, losing support through the introduction of the *community charge* and (within the Conservative Party in Parliament) through her hostility to the growing importance of Europe.
- Thatcher was challenged for the party leadership in November 1990 after Sir Geoffrey Howe, the Deputy Prime Minister, resigned in protest at her stance on Europe. Although not defeated by the challenger, *Heseltine*, the episode lost her the confidence of a majority of the *Cabinet* and she resigned.

Thatcherism: a set of policies and values associated with Margaret *Thatcher,* stressing a return to pre-1945 ideas on the economy and society.

- It was not an ideology thought out in advance, before Thatcher won office in 1979, but rather a series of responses to problems faced by Britain. Thatcherism stressed the importance of strong leadership and had a popular following among large sections of the electorate, including working-class voters who had not been traditionally Conservative.
- On the economy, Thatcherism set out to encourage private enterprise and reduce government involvement. It aimed to curb the runaway *inflation* of the 1970s and to pass laws to reduce trade union power. Features of economic policy included tax cuts for people with higher incomes, the reform of spending on the *welfare state* and the *privatisation* of industries and services.
- Thatcher and her closest colleagues, such as Norman Tebbit and Cecil Parkinson, stressed the importance of individual effort. Thatcherites were strongly critical of dependence on state assistance and of the moral climate associated with the *permissive society* of the 1960s.
- In external policy, Thatcherism involved a clear-cut patriotism, demonstrated in the handling of the *Falklands War, 1982*. Later, following Thatcher's September 1988 Bruges speech, it became associated with a more sceptical attitude towards European integration. This was in spite of her earlier support for the *Single European Act, 1985–86*. 'Euro-scepticism' survived her replacement by *Major* and contributed to the divisions that plagued the party in the 1990s.

think tank: a group of advisers employed by a government or political party to develop ideas for new policies.

- Think tanks have been largely a feature of post-1945 governments, several of which have looked beyond the traditional Civil Service for advice.
- Some have been based in Number 10, Downing Street, and have worked directly for the Prime Minister. An example is the Central Policy Review Staff, created by *Heath* in 1971 and abolished in 1983. Others, such as the Adam Smith Institute, a pro-free market group, have retained more political independence but have had some influence when a sympathetic government is in power.

Tolpuddle Martyrs: a group of Dorset farm labourers who were prosecuted in 1834 for taking an illegal oath of loyalty to a trade union.

t

- At this time, the legal status of trade unions was still uncertain. The authorities, who had faced the *Captain Swing riots* among farm labourers in 1830–31, were suspicious of working-class organisation. The Home Secretary, *Melbourne*, took a hard line.
- The labourers were sentenced to *transportation* to Australia for 7 years. This was seen as a harsh punishment for men who had behaved in a peaceful way. They were pardoned in 1836 and allowed to return to Britain.
- The Tolpuddle Martyrs were celebrated as pioneers of the trade union movement. A museum of trade union history was built in the village.

Tory Party: the forerunner of the *Conservative Party*. It began in the late seventeenth century and was associated with opposition to political reform.

- The name 'Tory' was originally a term of abuse. It means an Irish bandit and was used to describe the group who struggled to protect the right of Charles II's Catholic brother, James, to inherit the throne in the 1670s and 1680s.
- Tories were staunch defenders of the old constitution, based on the *Anglican Church*. They supported James not because he was Catholic, but because he was the legitimate heir to the throne.
- The label became widely used for supporters of the *Liverpool* government of 1812–27. Tories typically were Anglican country gentlemen who wished to uphold traditional patterns of authority. After the loss of power to the *Whigs* and the passing of the *Franchise Act, 1832,* the Tories were transformed into the Conservative Party.

TIP You need to be clear about how the Tories differed from their Whig opponents in terms of ideas and the nature of their support.

trade boards: institutions created by *Asquith*'s Liberal government in 1909 to regulate wages and hours in the low-paid sweated trades.

- Sweated trades included tailoring, lace making and chain making. They were poorly paid, repetitive tasks carried out mainly by female workers. They did not have trade union protection and the law had largely ignored them in the nineteenth century.
- Trade boards set minimum wages and maximum hours for workers in these trades.

TIP This is an example of the *New Liberalism* in practice.

Trade Disputes Act, 1927: a law passed by *Baldwin*'s government to restrict the activities of trade unions.

- The trade unions had been defeated in the *General Strike, 1926*. The act set out to ensure that they would not be in a position to challenge the government again.
- It banned sympathetic strikes in support of workers in other industries. Civil servants were banned from joining unions affiliated to the *Trades Union Congress.*
- The system whereby the *Labour Party* was funded from the political levy, contributed by trade unionists (see *Osborne judgement, 1909*), was changed.

From now on, an individual trade union member had positively to 'contract in' to pay the levy, otherwise it would not be deducted from his or her union subscription.

- The act was seen as a vindictive attack on the Labour movement and was repealed (cancelled) by the *Attlee* government in 1946.

Trades Disputes Act, 1906: see *Taff Vale Case, 1900–01*.

Trades Union Congress (TUC): the central organisation representing British trade unions, founded in 1868.

- The TUC's governing body, the General Council, gained increasing influence over *Labour Party* policy from the 1920s. This was because the trade unions were the largest subscribers to the party's funds.
- An important example of TUC influence was the party's commitment to *nationalisation*, which was expected to ensure that industries were run more fairly from the workers' point of view.
- TUC influence reached its peak in the 1960s and 1970s, when Labour governments consulted it over pay policy and other issues — an arrangement known in the popular press as 'beer and sandwiches at Number 10'. This ceased after the election of the *Thatcher* government, which set out to pass laws reducing trade union power.

Trade Union Act, 1913: see *Osborne judgement, 1909*.

transportation: the shipping of convicts to Australia or America, used as an alternative to prison or execution between the mid-seventeenth century and 1868.

- Australia was the main destination for convicts under the transportation system. It offered a possibility of a new start, although conditions aboard the prison ships were notoriously harsh.
- The practice was abolished in 1868.

triple (industrial) alliance: an alliance of Britain's three most powerful trade unions — the miners, transport workers and railwaymen — negotiated in 1914–15.

- The coming together of these three unions raised fears of a general strike and lent credibility to the belief that *syndicalism* was a serious threat to economic and social stability.
- In fact, the unions were concerned with wages and conditions, not with disruption for political ends, and the alliance did not come into action during the First World War.
- When it was activated, in April 1921, the alliance broke down. The transport workers and railwaymen decided not to support the miners in a dispute with the coal-mine owners. This was known as 'Black Friday'.

▨ *TIP* You need to know about the triple alliance in order to answer questions on the *Strange Death of Liberal England* theory.

Troubles: the name given to the revival of Catholic/Protestant conflict in Northern Ireland after 1968.

- Catholics in Northern Ireland were the victims of discrimination in jobs, housing, policing and other areas. The government set up in Stormont (a suburb of Belfast) after the *Anglo–Irish Treaty, 1921* was dominated by the representatives of the Protestant *Ulster Unionist Party*.
- In 1968–69, violence flared after Catholic community leaders organised demonstrations to demand equal civil rights with Protestants. The British government sent troops to keep order in 1969.
- The *IRA* revived under the guise of protecting the Catholic community and soon targeted British soldiers and law enforcers. This led to 30 years of conflict in Northern Ireland.
- The *Sunningdale Agreement, 1973*, the *Anglo–Irish Agreement, 1985* and the *Good Friday Agreement, 1998* were attempts to deal with the violence of the Troubles.

TIP The causes of the Troubles are essential for the AQA unit on 'Britain and Ireland, 1969–98'.

TUC: see *Trades Union Congress*.

two-power standard: see *Naval Defence Act, 1889*.

Ulster: historically, the most northerly of the four provinces of Ireland (Connacht, Leinster and Munster being the others). It has been equated with the political unit of Northern Ireland, a part of the UK, since the *Anglo–Irish Treaty, 1921*.

- Ulster has had a distinctive character since the seventeenth century, when the arrival of large numbers of settlers (especially from Scotland) gave it a Protestant majority.
- It was the only area of Ireland to experience the *Industrial Revolution*, and became a centre of the linen and shipbuilding industries, making it more prosperous than the rest of Ireland.
- It was a centre of resistance to the *Home Rule* Bills of 1886, 1893 and 1912. Ulster refused to consider incorporation into a united Ireland with a Catholic-dominated parliament in Dublin.
- The determination of a majority of Ulster's people to remain in the UK ensured that the island was partitioned between North and South in 1921.

Ulster Crisis, 1912–14: a situation of near civil war in Ireland, caused by the determination of Ulster's people to resist the *Home Rule* Bill proposed by the *Asquith* government.

- The passing of the 1911 *Parliament Act* by the Liberal government meant that the Home Rule Bill, introduced in the *House of Commons* in 1912, would automatically become law 2 years later. The *Irish Nationalist Party*, on whose votes the Liberal government depended, refused to consider the idea of excluding Ulster from Home Rule.
- The Ulster Protestant community, led by the lawyer and MP *Carson*, organised resistance to the threat of a Dublin parliament. They signed a mass petition, the Solemn League and Covenant, and began drilling the Ulster Volunteer Force. The *Conservative Party* leader, *Law*, gave his public support to the movement.
- The situation became more urgent in March 1914, when the so-called *Curragh mutiny* cast doubt on the willingness of British Army officers to obey government orders.
- Attempts to reach a compromise settlement failed. The Home Rule Bill became law in September 1914, but its operation was suspended for the duration of the First World War.

- Historians have been divided on the seriousness of the crisis. Some have argued that the government would have faced open rebellion had the First World War not intervened.

■ *TIP* The arguments for and against the seriousness of the Ulster Crisis are important for exam questions on Home Rule and on the *Strange Death of Liberal England.*

Ulster Unionist Party (also called 'the Official Unionist Party'): the main political party representing the Protestant community in Northern Ireland. It is committed to keeping Northern Ireland within the UK.

- The party evolved from the pre-1914 Ulster Unionist Council.
- It dominated the Stormont assembly in Belfast, which ran Northern Ireland between the *Anglo–Irish Treaty, 1921* and the introduction of *direct rule* in 1972.
- The party continued to represent the majority of the Protestant community in Northern Ireland during the *Troubles* of the 1960s–90s, although a hard-line grouping under *Paisley* left in 1971 to form the Democratic Unionist Party.
- The Ulster Unionist Party opposed concessions to the forces of Irish nationalism as represented by *Sinn Fein*. Under the leadership of David Trimble, however, a majority of the party agreed to support the *Good Friday Agreement, 1998* and to participate in the Northern Ireland assembly.

Ultras: hard-line members of the *Tory Party* in the 1820s who opposed political change, especially the granting of political rights to Roman Catholics and *nonconformists.*

- Ultras believed that any modification of the old constitution, dominated by the *Anglican Church,* would endanger national stability. They hated *Liberal Tories* such as *Canning.*
- They regarded the granting of *Catholic emancipation* in 1829 as a betrayal. One of their number, the Marquis of Winchilsea, challenged *Wellington* to a duel for having given in to Catholic pressure.
- A small number of Ultras, ironically, became converted to parliamentary reform in 1829–30, on the grounds that if more people had been allowed to vote, they would have stopped treacherous politicians from allowing Catholic emancipation.

■ *TIP* The importance of the Ultras lies in their contribution to the disintegration of the Tory Party between 1827 and 1830.

Unemployment Assistance Board: a body created by the *National Government* to deal with the problem of long-term unemployment during the *Great Depression* of the 1930s.

- Previously, unemployment benefit had been administered by Public Assistance Committees, controlled by local authorities.
- The government decided to hand over responsibility for unemployment benefit to a new central body in 1934, because there had been many local variations under the old system. The idea was that the new body would provide uniform scales of assistance, regardless of local political pressures.

- The introduction of the Unemployment Assistance Board was delayed until 1937 because of a dispute about the level of payments when it was first unveiled.

University Tests Act, 1871: an act passed by *Gladstone*'s first government that allowed non-Anglicans to teach at Oxford and Cambridge universities.

- Teaching at England's oldest universities had been monopolised by members of the Church of England (see *Anglican Church*) for centuries. The Gladstone government ended this monopoly, as part of its policy of opening up institutions to people on grounds of merit rather than privilege.
- Many scholarships, however, continued to be reserved for Anglicans.

▧ *TIP* The act illustrates one of the key principles of *Gladstonian Liberalism.*

utilitarianism: see *Benthamism.*

U-turn: a popular phrase to describe a politically embarrassing reversal of policy.

- U-turns have been performed by politicians long before the term was coined. The granting of *Catholic emancipation* in 1829 and the repeal of the *Corn Laws* in 1846 are examples from the early part of the period.
- Perhaps the classic example is *Heath*'s decision to provide state aid for failing industries, such as Rolls Royce in 1971, and to introduce an *incomes policy* in 1972–73. Critics argued that this contradicted the free-market position on which the Conservatives were elected in 1970.
- Margaret *Thatcher* made much of her determination not to change policy, famously declaring at the 1980 *Conservative Party* conference, 'You turn if you want to; the lady's not for turning'.

Vereeniging, Treaty of, 1902: the treaty that ended the *Anglo–Boer War, 1899–1902.*

- The treaty confirmed the British annexation (take-over) of the Boer republics of the Transvaal and the Orange Free State. On the other hand, it protected the use of the Boer language (Afrikaans) in schools and the law. To the satisfaction of the Boers, it also failed to grant political rights to the black population.
- The Liberal government granted self-government to the Transvaal and Orange Free State in 1906. In 1910, they combined to form the Union of South Africa, a British *Dominion.*

Versailles, Treaty of: see *Paris Peace Conference, 1919.*

Victoria, Queen (1819–1901; reigned 1837–1901): the longest-reigning British monarch, who presided over the slow transformation of royal power into a constitutional monarchy.

- Victoria succeeded her uncle, William IV, as monarch in 1837. The two main influences on the early part of her reign were her first Prime Minister, *Melbourne,* and her husband, Prince Albert of Saxe-Coburg-Gotha, whom she married in 1840.
- Albert's premature death in 1861 plunged her into deep mourning. Her withdrawal from public life was largely to blame for the growth of a republican movement in the 1860s and early 1870s.
- She was persuaded to return to a public, ceremonial role by *Disraeli.* He conferred the title of Empress of India on her in 1876.
- In old age, Victoria became the symbol of empire and a focus for national and imperial unity, celebrated with great pageantry in her Golden Jubilee of 1887 and Diamond Jubilee of 1897.
- Victoria had strong political prejudices and was particularly hostile to *Gladstone,* whom she viewed as unpatriotic and likely to endanger the interests of the empire. However, her political interventions were usually discreet and she knew when to give way.
- She was the first truly constitutional monarch. In her reign, royal power was limited by the growth of organised political parties and by movement towards democracy.

Vienna, Congress of, 1814–15: the peace conference that ended the *Napoleonic Wars*, attended by representatives of Britain, France, Austria, Russia and Prussia.

- Britain was represented by *Castlereagh*, whose main objectives were to re-create a *balance of power* after 20 years of continental war, and to advance Britain's overseas interests.
- In order to prevent a revival of French power, France was stripped of all the territories it had conquered since 1790.
- Belgium and Holland were merged to create a buffer against French expansion.
- Britain, Austria, Russia and Prussia signed the Quadruple Alliance and agreed to hold regular congresses (meetings) to discuss matters of mutual concern.
- Britain's standing as the world's main naval and commercial power was confirmed by the acquisition of a number of important bases: Malta and the Ionian Islands in the Mediterranean, and Heligoland in the North Sea. British power in the Indian Ocean was enhanced by gaining Mauritius, Ceylon (now Sri Lanka) and the Cape of Good Hope in southern Africa. British control of the West Indies sugar trade was increased by the acquisition of Tobago and St Lucia.

■ *TIP* Remember not merely to list Britain's gains in the Vienna settlement, but also to understand precisely how they furthered British interests.

welfare state: the idea that the state should take responsibility for ensuring a basic level of income and public services for the whole population.

● The foundations of a welfare state were laid by the Liberal governments of 1905–14, which introduced *old age pensions* and *National Insurance*. The idea of comprehensive welfare cover did not, however, arrive until the *Beveridge Report, 1942*.

● Some features of the welfare state were introduced by Winston *Churchill*'s wartime government: the *Education Act, 1944* and family allowances, later known as child benefit, in 1945.

● The most important work was done by the *Attlee* government of 1945–51. Comprehensive National Insurance was introduced in 1946. National Assistance (later known as supplementary benefit) was introduced to top up the incomes of the very poor, who could not afford to make insurance contributions. In 1948 the *National Health Service (NHS)* was created.

● All three main parties accepted the main principles of the welfare state. Its rising costs, however, became a cause of concern in the final quarter of the twentieth century.

Wellington (Arthur Wellesley), 1st Duke of (1769–1852): a leading British general and victor of the Battle of Waterloo, 1815; Master General of the Ordnance 1819–27; Prime Minister 1828–30; Foreign Secretary 1834–35; Minister without Portfolio 1841–46.

● Wellington's military career in the *Napoleonic Wars* earned him a national reputation.

● In politics, he associated with the right wing of the *Tory Party*.

● He became Prime Minister after the early death of *Canning* and the failure of *Goderich* to form a stable government.

● He failed to unite the party, losing *Huskisson* and the *Liberal Tories* from his government in a dispute over the redistribution of two parliamentary seats in 1828. He was also seen as a traitor by the right-wing *Ultras* for granting *Catholic emancipation* in 1829.

● His refusal to contemplate parliamentary reform left his government isolated, and he resigned in November 1830.

- In later life, he was a loyal supporter of *Peel*.
- Wellington was mourned as a national hero on his death in 1852.
- **TIP** The events of Wellington's premiership are important for an understanding of how the *Whig* government of 1830–41 came about.

Welsh National Party (Plaid Cymru): a political party, founded in 1925, that campaigns for independence for Wales.

- The party made little impression before a by-election victory in 1966. It has grown in importance since the two general elections of 1974.
- It draws its support mainly from rural, central and northern Wales.
- The election of a Labour government in 1997 brought about the establishment of a Welsh assembly in Cardiff, which was welcomed by Welsh nationalists.

wet Tory: a term of abuse used by supporters of Margaret *Thatcher,* to describe Conservatives who were too inclined to compromise with the ideas of their Labour opponents.

- 'Wet' Tories saw themselves as heirs to a tradition of *paternalism* in Conservative thought, stretching back through *Macmillan* to *Disraeli* in the nineteenth century. They regarded Thatcherites ('dries') as too rigid and extreme, and likely to divide society through their drive to curb *inflation* at the expense of jobs and public services.
- On her appointment as Prime Minister in 1979, Thatcher at first felt obliged, for the sake of party unity, to give government posts to some of the 'wets'. They included James Prior, Employment Secretary 1979–81, and Ian Gilmour, deputy Foreign Secretary in the same period.
- In the autumn of 1981, Thatcher removed the leading wets and promoted more like-minded 'dry' Conservatives such as Norman Tebbit (Employment Secretary 1981–83).

Whig Party: an aristocratic, pro-reform party, with its origins in the seventeenth century, which evolved into the *Liberal Party* between the 1830s and the 1860s.

- The name is derived from the word 'Whiggamore', a Scottish term for a rebel. It was a term of abuse, used by their *Tory* opponents.
- A handful of aristocratic families (for example, those of *Grey* and *Russell*) provided the nucleus of the Whig Party. They saw themselves as guardians of the 'Glorious Revolution' of 1688, when James II was removed from the throne and Parliament placed limitations on the power of the monarchy.
- Whigs believed in the right of an enlightened, landowning élite to govern in the interests of the people. They maintained that by an intelligent reading of public opinion, they could make timely changes that would avert more drastic upheavals. The passing of the *Franchise Act, 1832* is an example of this approach.
- In the early nineteenth century, Whigs built links with the commercial and professional middle classes and took up the cause of religious toleration for *nonconformists*. This provided the basis for the emerging Liberal Party.
- Whigs continued to exercise influence in the Liberal governments of *Gladstone*. They tended to act as a check on the desire of *Radicals* for rapid and far-reaching

reforms. Most of the Whigs left the Liberal Party and became *Liberal Unionists* following the Irish *Home Rule* crisis of 1886.

whip: one of a team of MPs charged with ensuring that members of a parliamentary party vote in the way required by the leadership.

- The Chief Whip is not a member of the *Cabinet*, but attends its meetings because of the importance of party discipline in the *House of Commons*. He or she has an office in Number 12, Downing Street, close to the official residences of the Prime Minister and the Chancellor of the Exchequer.
- The first whips served in the early nineteenth century, although they lacked official status. Until the early twentieth century, the Chief Whip was responsible for his party's organisation in the country as well as at Westminster. Thus, Herbert Gladstone, Liberal Chief Whip, negotiated the *Lib–Lab Pact, 1903*.
- The term 'whip' is also used to describe a written instruction circulated to inform MPs of forthcoming votes in which they will be expected to take part.

Whitelaw, William (1918–99): Lord President of the Council 1970–72; Northern Ireland Secretary 1972–73; Employment Secretary 1973–74; Home Secretary 1979–83; leader of the Lords 1983–88.

- As the first Northern Ireland Secretary, Whitelaw opened negotiations with the *IRA* and prepared for the *Sunningdale Agreement, 1973*.
- He was a contender for the *Conservative Party* leadership in 1975, but lost to *Thatcher* and thereafter became her loyal deputy.
- He was widely respected by Conservatives of all shades of opinion (and by members of other parties), and was credited with providing essential support for the first two Thatcher governments. He was regarded as a force for stability and common sense.

wholehoggers: see *free fooders*.

Willis's Rooms meeting, 1859: see *Liberal Party*.

Wilson, Harold (1916–95): President of the Board of Trade 1947–51; Prime Minister 1964–70, 1974–76; leader of the *Labour Party* 1963–76.

- Wilson was an Oxford economist and wartime civil servant who rose rapidly on commencing a political career in 1945.
- He earned a reputation as a left-winger — to which he did not live up in later life — when he resigned from the *Attlee* government in company with *Bevan* in 1951.
- Elected Labour leader in 1963, he presented the party as a dynamic force and his Conservative opponent, *Douglas-Home,* as out of date. Wilson took office in October 1964 with promises of modernisation and economic regeneration through a 'national plan'.
- His 1964–70 government disappointed many with its failure to break the cycle of *stop–go* economics. Embarrassments over *devaluation of the pound, Rhodesia* and '*In Place of Strife'* proposals marked this period of office.
- In his second term as Prime Minister, Wilson had to cope with the leftward movement of the Labour Party and with internal division over entry into the

EEC. He held the party together through the device of a *referendum* on Europe in 1975. He retired unexpectedly in April 1976.

■ *TIP* Any assessment of Wilson as Prime Minister needs to take into account the difficulties he faced in maintaining the unity of the Labour Party.

'wind of change' speech, 1960: a speech by *Macmillan* to the South African Parliament in Cape Town, in which he spoke of nationalism as a 'wind of change' blowing through the African continent.

● The speech was delivered in February 1960 during a tour of Africa. It signalled Britain's realistic acceptance of African nationalism as a political fact and indicated that Macmillan's government would follow a policy of *decolonisation.*

● It was a warning to his audience, the South African government, which was trying to maintain a policy of apartheid (separate development for black and white people), under which the black population was denied political rights.

'winter of discontent', 1978–79: a period of strikes which damaged the image of *Callaghan*'s Labour government and prepared the way for the Conservative victory in the general election of May 1979.

● Callaghan had tried to implement an *incomes policy* under which trade unions were to accept a national wage increase limit of 5%. Public-sector workers rejected this and there was a wave of strikes.

● Images of uncollected rubbish and locked graveyards appeared in the media. This helped the Conservatives by suggesting that the unions had too much power. Callaghan was further damaged when he tried to play down the situation on returning from a conference abroad. His words were turned into the newspaper headline, 'Crisis? What crisis?' This appeared complacent and out of touch with the realities of life in Britain during a hard winter.

Women's Social and Political Union (WSPU): an organisation founded by the *Pankhursts* in 1903, more militant than earlier women's pressure groups, to campaign for votes for women.

● WSPU members were known as *suffragettes.*

● The suffragettes drew attention to their cause by disrupting political meetings and attacking property and public buildings. In 1913, one suffragette, Emily Davison, threw herself under the King's horse at the Epsom Derby.

● When arrested, suffragettes often went on hunger strike in prison. When the authorities forcibly fed them, this made the women appear the victims of an unsympathetic, repressive government. The so-called *Cat and Mouse Act, 1913,* passed by the *Asquith* government, was widely condemned.

● The WSPU campaign was suspended on the outbreak of war in 1914.

● The tactics of the WSPU were controversial. Some argued that they put pressure on the government by attracting publicity. Others said that their extreme tactics put off people who might have been sympathetic to their cause.

■ *TIP* You need to be aware of the arguments regarding the effectiveness (or otherwise) of the WSPU.

W

Woolton (Frederick Marquis), 1st Earl of (1883–1964): Minister of Food 1940–43; Minister of Reconstruction 1943–45; Lord President of the Council 1951–52; Chancellor of the Duchy of Lancaster 1952–55; chairman of the *Conservative Party* 1946–55.

● Woolton was a successful businessman who entered government during the Second World War. As Minister of Food, he superintended the rationing programme and publicised the need for sacrifices by the British public. He was popularly associated with the wartime economy measure of the 'Woolton pie'.

● As chairman of the Conservative Party after its crushing defeat in the 1945 general election, he organised major fund-raising and membership drives. He reorganised the party in readiness for the 1951 election, which it won.

workhouse system: see *New Poor Law, 1834*.

Workmen's Compensation Acts, 1897 and 1906: laws that enabled workers to claim compensation from their employers for industrial injuries.

● These acts spared workers the costs of launching a private court case, which was usually beyond their means.

● The 1897 act, passed by the *Salisbury* government, made employers liable for injuries sustained in mines, factories, quarries and railways. The 1906 act, passed by the *Campbell-Bannerman* government, extended it to other trades and made possible claims for industrially related diseases.

● A more comprehensive scheme was introduced as part of the *Attlee* government's 1946 *National Insurance* legislation.

▩ *TIP* The 1897 act, associated with *Joseph Chamberlain*, is one of a small number of social reforms passed by Conservative governments under Lord Salisbury.

'workshop of the world': a popular description of Britain's position as the world's leading industrial, trading and banking centre between about 1850 and 1873.

● In this period, Britain was the most important producer of cotton, coal, iron and ships. A world-wide network of trade, with guaranteed markets in the *British empire,* made this possible. Policies of *free trade,* adopted by British governments in this period, allowed the entry of cheap raw materials and suited the interests of British business.

● The City of London was the world's leading centre for banking and insurance, and played a major role in financing these developments.

● Britain was the first nation to undergo an *Industrial Revolution* and potential rivals, especially Germany and the USA, did not begin to compete seriously until the mid-1870s.

▩ *TIP* It is important to know the reasons why Britain enjoyed such a lead over its rivals in the mid-nineteenth century.

WSPU: see *Women's Social and Political Union*.

Young England: a romantic *Tory* political movement, active in the mid-1840s in opposition to *Peel*'s government.

- There were few members of the group, but they drew attention to themselves by their speeches and writings. The most important member was *Disraeli*.
- Young England's ideas were backward-looking. They were based on dislike of the *Industrial Revolution* and of the money-making culture of nineteenth-century Britain. They preferred an older, idealised way of life whereby the upper classes took responsibility for the poor in a paternalistic way.
- The group had a short existence, dissolving after its members voted in different ways on the *Maynooth* issue in 1845.

■ *TIP* Beware of making strong connections between the ideas of Young England and Disraeli's social reforms as prime minister in 1874–80.

Young Ireland: an Irish nationalist group, active between 1841 and 1847, which split from *O'Connell* to plan a rebellion against Britain.

- The group was led by Charles Gavan Duffy, Thomas Davis and John Dillon, and had its own journal, ***The Nation***.
- It rejected the peaceful nationalism associated with O'Connell and formed the Irish Confederation in 1847. It declined in importance after a failed attempt at rebellion against British rule later that year.

Zimbabwe: see *Rhodesia*.

Zinoviev letter, 1924: a message to the British Communist Party, purporting to be from Zinoviev, president of the Moscow-based organisation Communist International, which was released shortly before the October 1924 general election.

● The letter urged British workers to take part in action to destabilise the state. It was printed in the British press and was widely believed because of current fears of Soviet *communism*. The communist revolution in Russia had taken place 7 years earlier.

● The letter had implications for the Labour government of *MacDonald,* which had earlier given official recognition to the Soviet government. It may have played a part in preventing Labour from being re-elected, although most historians argue that it would have lost, even without the appearance of the letter.

● It now seems almost certain that the letter was forged by a Russian exile and was leaked by members of the British security services who wanted to damage Labour.

Zulu War, 1879: a conflict between British forces and the Zulus, a black warrior race in southern Africa.

● The Zulus had a kingdom to the north of the British colony of Natal in southern Africa. Sir Bartle Frere, the British High Commissioner in the region, considered that they presented a challenge to the extension of British power.

● Without the authorisation of the *Disraeli* government, Frere embarked on a policy of confrontation with the Zulus. The British were defeated by a Zulu army at Isandhlwana in January 1879. A British force held out against overwhelming numbers in the missionary station at Rorke's Drift, an episode later made famous in the film *Zulu*. Finally, the Zulus were defeated at Ulundi in July 1879.

● Although the war led to the dismantling of the Zulu kingdom, the early reverses caused embarrassment for the Disraeli government. Government policy was attacked by *Gladstone* in the *Midlothian campaigns* prior to the general election of April 1880.

Appendix
Modules/Units covered in this *Essential Word Dictionary*
Advanced Subsidiary (AS)

AQA

Britain, 1815–41
Britain, 1895–1918
The Industrial Revolution: change and opportunity in the economy and society, c.1750–1830
Britain, 1929–1951
Aspects of British History, 1815–41
Aspects of British History, 1895–1921
Aspects of Economic and Social History, 1832–48

Edexcel

Poverty and the British State, c. 1815–50
Votes for Women, c. 1880–1918
The Younger Pitt: national revival and the impact of revolution, 1783–1801
The age of the railway, 1830–1914
Welfare and the Constitution: the Liberal governments, 1905–15
Parliamentary reform, 1815–50
The Health of the People: public health and social policy, 1832–75
Responding to Reform: party and policy in the age of Gladstone and Disraeli, 1867–85
Conflict, Depression and Opportunity: British society between the wars, 1919–39

OCR

The Condition of England, 1832–53
The Irish Question in the Age of Parnell, 1877–94
England in a New Century, 1900–18
England, 1780–1846
Britain, 1846–1906
Britain, 1899–1964

Advanced (A2)

AQA

Britain, 1841–1914
Britain, 1918–51
Maturity, Change and Crisis in the British Economy and Society, c.1830–1914
Britain, 1951–97
Britain and the Scramble for Africa, 1880–95
Changes in the Provision of Education, 1918–51
Public Health: problems and policies, 1830–1914
Great Britain and Appeasement in the 1930s
Britain and Ireland, 1969–98

Edexcel

Tory Men and Tory Measures: the age of Lord Liverpool, 1815–27
The Age of Peel, 1832–46
Conservative Supremacy: policies and parties in Britain, 1886–1906
The Road to War: British foreign policy, 1890–1914
From Peace to Appeasement: British foreign policy between the wars
Medicine in Britain in the Twentieth Century, c.1890 –c.1990
Britain and Decolonisation, c.1870–1980
Representation and Democracy in Britain, 1830–1931
The State and the Poor in Britain, c.1830–1939
Chartism
Decline of the Liberal Party, c.1900–29

OCR

Gladstone and Disraeli, 1846–80
Britain and Germany, 1933–39
Britain and Ireland, 1798–1921
War and Society in Britain, 1793–1918
Poor Law to Welfare State, 1834–1948
The Development of Democracy, 1868–1992
The Development of the Mass Media, 1896–1996